Practical GRC

GOVERNANCE RISK COMPLIANCE

Implementation

CYBERSECURITY - AUDITOR'S VIEW

Practical GRC

GOVERNANCE RISK COMPLIANCE

Implementation

CYBERSECURITY - AUDITOR'S VIEW

By Santosh Desai & Gauri Saple

SHROFF PUBLISHERS & DISTRIBUTORS PVT. LTD
Navi Mumbai

Practical GRC Implementation: Cybersecurity - Auditor's View

By Santosh Desai & Gauri Saple

First Edition: July 2025

ISBN: 978-93-6808-464-8

Printed at Decora Book Prints Pvt. Ltd. Mumbai • Published by Shroff Publishers and Distributors Pvt. Ltd. B-103, Railway Commercial Complex, Sector 3, Sanpada (E), Navi Mumbai 400705 • Tel: (91 22) 4158 4158 WhatsApp +91 7304487700 4158 4141 • E-mail: spdorders@shroffpublishers.com • URL: www.shroffpublishers.com

Preface

Unlocking the Power of GRC: A Practical Guide to Governance, Risk, and Compliance

In today's digital-first world, organizations face a growing need to build secure, structured, and compliant IT environments. This is where Governance, Risk, and Compliance (GRC) comes into play - a powerful framework that integrates people, processes, and technologies to ensure that IT operations align with business goals while managing risk and meeting regulatory obligations. At its core, GRC enables organizations to:

- Identify and mitigate technology and user-related risks
- Protect data confidentiality, integrity, and availability
- Comply with regulatory standards and industry best practices
- Establish governance across business functions with traceable IT alignment

As data volumes soar and regulatory scrutiny increases, IT audits and assessments have become central to maintaining trust and operational efficiency. A modern audit approach must be risk-based, structured, and pragmatic - mapping technical controls to regulatory requirements while ensuring effective collaboration between auditors and auditees.

This book is designed to offer real-world insights into how GRC is implemented, audited, and optimized in dynamic business environments. Each chapter walks you through critical audit domains with:

- Practical information-gathering templates
- High-level policy structures
- Realistic audit walkthroughs based on live case studies
- Step-by-step workflow guidance for delivering audit services with minimal friction

We begin with an introduction to GRC and its value in modern IT ecosystems, followed by:

- The need for a unified and integrated GRC framework
- The benefits of automation in driving consistency and efficiency
- A deep dive into each domain of Information Security Management Systems (ISMS)
- And finally, an exploration of the **GRC-as-a-Service (GRCaaS)** model - a future-forward approach to scalable compliance and risk management

Whether you are a **GRC professional, auditor,** or **IT leader,** this book will help you navigate the complexities of today's regulatory landscape with confidence and clarity.

Let's build better, smarter, and more secure systems — **the GRC way.**

Some Quotes by Authors

"Adoption of "Risk based – Holistic – Pragmatic – Dynamic" Approach enables implementation of structured GRC program"

"Too many security controls do not mean good deployment of security".

"Prevention through contextual monitoring is more important instead of just deployment controls"

"if you don't see it, it doesn't exist" the ostrich effect does not work"

"Defence in depth should enable deployment of collaborative and flexible security program without making it rigid and bureaucratic

Authors: Santosh Desai and Gauri Saple

Contributor: Harshil Kothari

Table of Content

7. GRC AND ACCESS MANAGEMENT

8. GRC AND THREAT VULNERABILITY MANAGEMENT

9. GRC AND IT-OT ASSESSMENT

10. GRC AND EVENT AND LOG MANAGEMENT

FIGURES

Chapter

1

GRC (Governance-Risk-Compliance) Three Pillars of Information System Security Program

1. Introduction

In today's fast-paced digital landscape, enterprise business processes are increasingly powered by next-generation technologies - including **Generative AI, Automation,** and **Multi-cloud environments**. These advancements bring significant operational efficiencies and real-time insights. However, they also introduce complexity and heightened risk to the IT ecosystem.

Modern enterprise environments are no longer confined by geography. Data - once seen through the lens of **"GIGO" (Garbage In, Garbage Out)** - has now become the **new oil,** fuelling rapid decision-making and high-performance computing. At the same time, organizations operate across hybrid infrastructures, combining **traditional data centers, public/private clouds,** and a blend of **wired and wireless technologies,** making security and governance more challenging than ever.

A Complex Threat Landscape

With increasing **globalization, Industry 4.0/5.0 adoption,** and the expansion of digital services, organizations must navigate a rising tide of **cyber threats.** Threat actors - both internal and external - are exploiting vulnerabilities across a sprawling and interconnected digital surface. Protecting organizational assets now requires looking beyond the traditional **CIA triad** (**C**onfidentiality, **I**ntegrity, and **A**vailability).

We must now also focus on:

- **The fourth dimension: Data Privacy,** critical for compliance with data protection laws
- **The fifth dimension: Safety,** especially vital in **Operational Technology (OT)** environments

The Role of GRC in Today's Enterprises

To manage this complexity, organizations must adopt a globally aligned and scalable approach to Information Security. This calls for implementing a robust **Governance, Risk, and Compliance (GRC)** framework. A well-defined GRC framework ensures:

- **Governance:** Strategic alignment between IT and business goals, with clearly defined roles, responsibilities, and decision-making structures
- **Risk Management:** Proactive identification and mitigation of risks related to technology, people, and processes
- **Compliance**: Adherence to applicable laws, regulations, and industry standards (regional and global)

By embracing GRC, organizations can:

- Streamline digital operations
- Standardize control implementation
- Align IT initiatives with business imperatives
- Build resilience against emerging cyber and operational risks

The following provides a broad definition of the terms **Governance – Risk – Compliance**

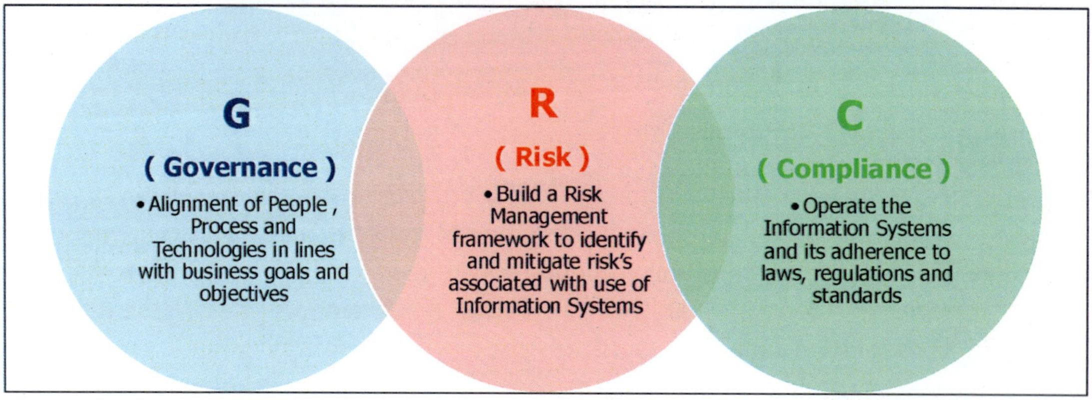

Figure 1- Governance – Risk – Compliance – Managing IT and Management

Conclusion

In essence, GRC is no longer optional - it is the foundational layer of any modern Information System Security Program. As organizations move towards hyper-connected, AI-enabled environments, the integration of GRC across all layers of technology and operations is key to achieving secure, compliant, and sustainable digital transformation.

2. Benefits of adoption of GRC framework

Adopting a **Governance, Risk, and Compliance (GRC)** framework using a **top-down approach** empowers organizations to proactively manage risks, align IT with business goals, and ensure compliance with regulatory obligations. Most importantly, it helps build **trust and credibility** with customers, partners, regulators, and other key stakeholders.

A well-integrated GRC framework does more than just safeguard data and systems - it enables informed decision-making, operational transparency, and strategic agility. By involving professionals across all business tiers and functions, organizations can address both **vertical (department-specific)** and **horizontal (cross-functional)** risk and compliance needs.

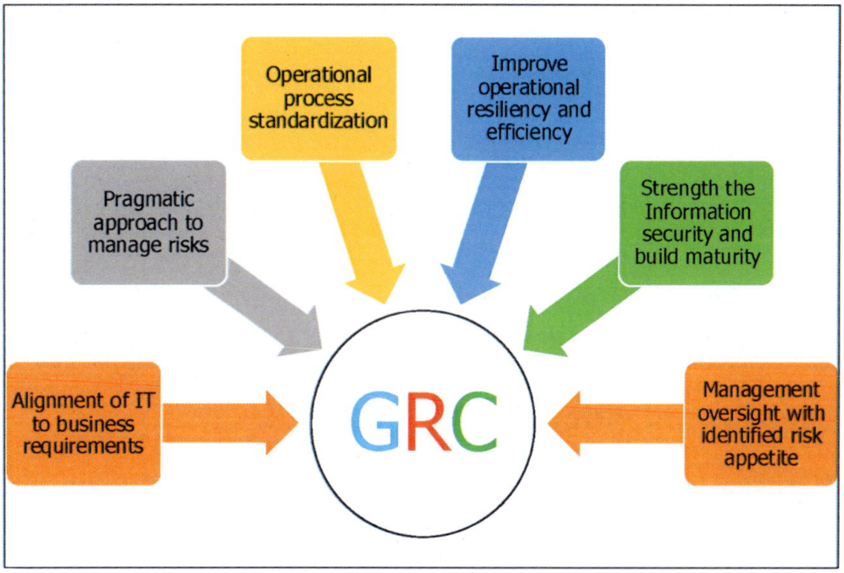

Figure 2 GRC- Benefits

By embracing the GRC framework, organizations not only protect their digital assets but also drive value creation, innovation, and sustainable growth. In the next section, we will explore the **core components and structure** of a mature GRC framework.

3. Negatives impact of non GRC framework

Despite its strategic importance, many organizations still perceive **GRC implementation** as a **cost center** or a mere **audit formality.** This limited view leads to minimal investment, lack of integration, and a siloed approach - all of which expose the organization to significant business, operational, and reputational risks.

In today's interconnected and highly regulated digital ecosystem, failing to implement a structured GRC framework can result in **costly consequences.**

- **Reputational Impact -** Global business requires demonstration of good practices. Absence of same will straight away impact business relationship with global partners, customers, stake holders resulting in loss of reputation, trust as well business opportunities
- **Non-Compliance –** failure to adhere to requirements of regulations and laws will result in penalties and fines
- **Ad hoc operations –** Absence of structured environment will result in ad hoc mode of functions, resulting in disruptions of services, non-co-ordination between teams
- **No transparency –** Operations may work in silos, resulting in operational inefficiency and lack of visibility, leading to reactive approach and thus more disruptions
- **No Risk Mitigation –** In today's digital world identifying potential risks to information assets is of top importance, failure to proactively identify, detect, prevent and dither may result in compromise of information, data loss, and data leakage
- **No Audit –** Absence of ongoing audits and assessment, may leave gaps unidentified, which may result in cyber-attacks from different threat actors

4. GRC and Organizational Risk

Modern **enterprise information systems and technology operations** are no longer confined to internal policies alone - they are subject to a wide array of **global standards, regional regulations,** and **industry-specific compliance requirements.** Each industry vertical - whether financial services, healthcare, manufacturing, or critical infrastructure - has unique cybersecurity expectations that require tailored control environments and risk responses.

To manage these complex and multi-dimensional risks, organizations need to move beyond reactive compliance checklists and adopt a holistic, integrated, and dynamic GRC framework.

- **Compliance Risk** – risk to organization arising out of regional regulatory requirement adherence, and alignment with global adopted standards such ISO/IEC, COBIT, SOC 2
- **Technology Risk** – risk to organization due to usage of various digital technology platforms and needs to adherence to best industry standard practices
- **Operational Risk** – risk to organization arising of its requirement to follow ITIL operational framework
- **Brand Risk** – risk to organization's reputation and brand image due to possible cyber-attacks and making the system unavailable

The implementation of a **Governance, Risk, and Compliance (GRC)** framework lays a strong foundation for building **robust Information System (IS) controls** - encompassing **policies, processes, and procedures.** These foundational elements are then **mapped to corresponding Information Technology (IT), Operational Technology (OT),** and Industrial Internet of Things **(IIoT)** controls to ensure seamless integration across the organization's digital ecosystem.

GRC not only guides the formulation of governance principles but also drives the deployment of **technical security controls** across various layers.

- **Perimeter Security Controls** – Firewalls, IDS/IPS, VPNs
- **Content Security Controls** – DLP, anti-malware, email/web filtering
- **Communication & Data Security Controls** – Encryption, secure protocols, access controls

By aligning **IS Governance** and **Data Security Governance** within a unified framework, organizations can establish a well-structured and scalable control environment that supports both **strategic business objectives and regulatory compliance mandates.** The following schematic demonstrates a typical top down structure of a GRC framework;

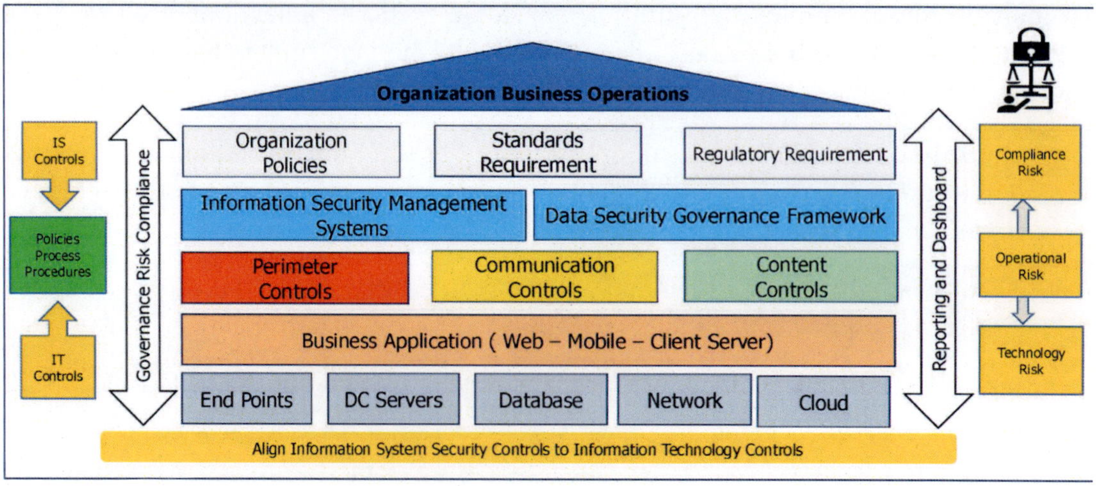

Figure 3 GRC Framework for Illustration only

Think of the **GRC framework as a house-like structure**, designed from **top to bottom** - each layer supporting the next to build a resilient and secure digital foundation for the organization.

At the Top (Roof)

This top level represents the **strategic alignment** with **business objectives**, **regulatory requirements**, and **global standards** (such as ISO 27001, NIST, GDPR, etc.). It ensures that the organization's GRC efforts are rooted in its overarching mission and compliance obligations.

Middle Layer (Walls and Structure)

This middle layer focuses on **Information System (IS) controls**, addressing both **Information Governance** and **Data Security Governance**. It defines the **policies, processes, and procedures** that guide how information is handled, accessed, stored, and protected across the organization.

Foundation Layer (Basement and Infrastructure)

At the base, the framework maps out the **technical IT security controls** - spanning IT, OT, and IIoT environments - to ensure the **Confidentiality, Integrity, and Availability (CIA)** of digital assets and other critical systems. These include firewalls, endpoint security, encryption, access control, and monitoring solutions.

Governance layer runs **horizontal and vertically** across different business functions using the digital business process implemented within HR, IT, Applications, Finance and other Departments

Risk layer runs **vertically** across IS and IT controls, comprising of applicability with deployment and with respect to its implementation covering all digital processes, associated IT assets and applications

Compliance maps IT with respect to the business objectives, monitoring regulators and global / regional standards and guidelines

This structured, **top-down GRC architecture** ensures that governance principles cascade effectively, from business strategy to operational controls, enabling organizations to **build trust, reduce risk, and sustain compliance** across a dynamic threat landscape.

5. Build GRC and Information Security Management System

Whether in an **IT (Information Technology)** or **OT (Operational Technology)** environment, organizations must adopt a **360-degree, structured approach** when building their GRC framework. A practical and effective method is the **A-D-A-M model**, which emphasizes four integrated phases to ensure a comprehensive implementation of GRC and **Information Security Management Systems (ISMS):**

- **Audit and Assessment (A)**
    - Understand organizations objectives and areas of pain
    - Review current digital environment,
    - Map requirements with respect to IS /OT controls and its priorities
    - Conduct Risk Assessment
- **Define and Develop (D)**
    - Build statement of applicability
    - Build policies, procedures, process in lines with regulations and standards requirement
    - Define organization wide roles and responsibilities, and build operational governance
    - Build operating templates and work instructions
    - Define KPI (Key Performance Indicators) and KRA (Key Result Areas) for different teams
    - Define the Risk appetite statements

- **Apply (A) and implement**
  - Deploy related technologies, IT security controls to secure the digital infrastructure deployed in the environment
  - Deploy monitoring and measurement controls
- **Manage (M) and Maintain**
  - Ongoing sustenance and running of program as part of continuous monitoring, and ongoing running an annual ISMS wheel
  - Regular and periodic audit and assessment
  - Conduct security awareness training sessions and build security culture

The **A-D-A-M** approach provides a 360-degree perspective to developing a robust GRC (Governance, Risk, and Compliance) framework. It emphasizes a proactive, structured methodology that helps organizations:

- Assess and understand risks at a granular level
- Detect and identify gaps across people, processes, and technologies
- Align and redefine operational and security requirements
- Maintain continuous improvement to enhance and mature the GRC posture

This approach is not a one-time exercise, but a cyclical process of enhancement that aligns with the evolving threat landscape, regulatory expectations, and business needs. In essence, the **A-D-A-M approach mirrors the Information Security Management System (ISMS) Wheel of Action**, where every stage feeds into the next, creating a continuous loop of improvement and assurance.

The schematic diagram below illustrates how the A-D-A-M approach and the ISMS wheel operate in tandem, reinforcing each other to build a resilient, compliant, and business-aligned security environment.

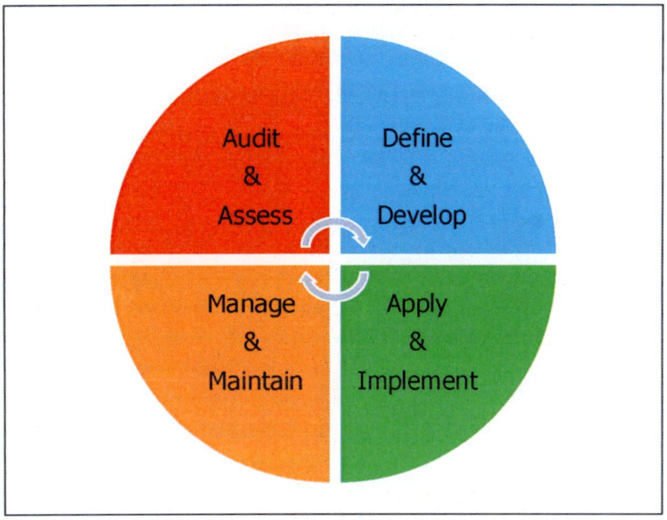

Audit & Assess

Current State Posture Review

Define & Develop

Build Policy Framework

Apply & Implement

Deploy Technology Platform

Manage & Maintain

Ongoing Support

Figure 4 ADAM Approach for GRC

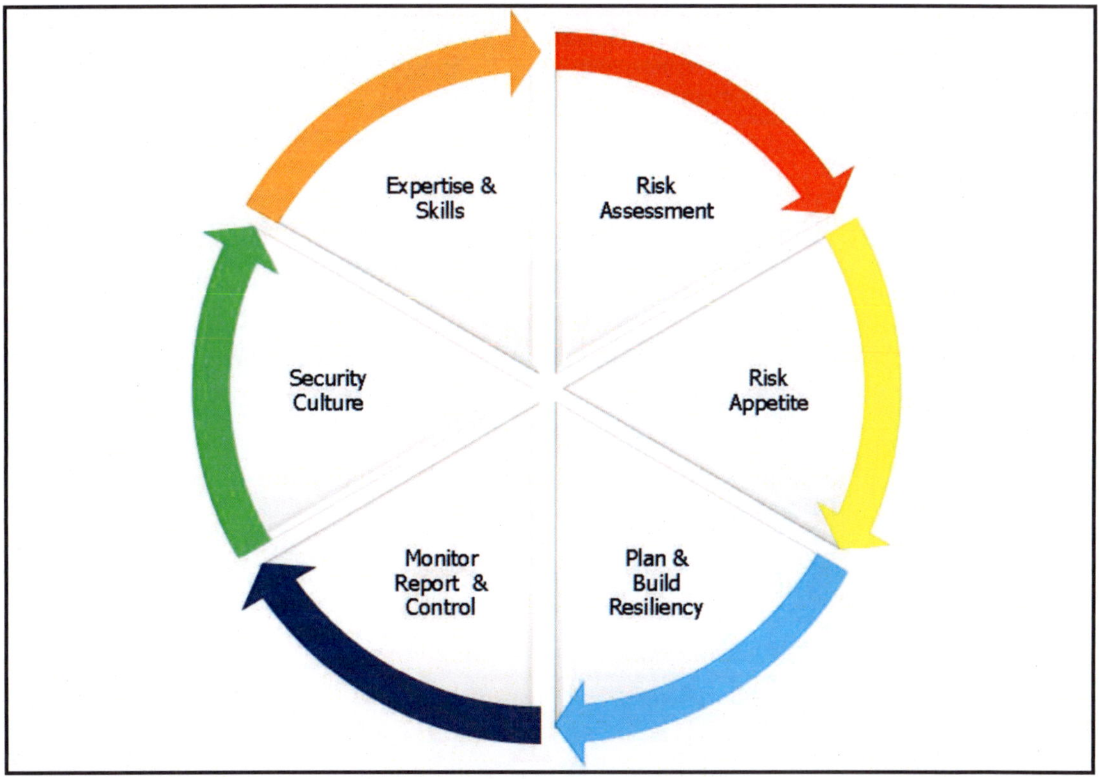

Figure 5 Annual ISMS Wheel

6. Conclusion

In today's **digitally driven world**, where data is a strategic asset, ensuring **Safety, Security, and Surveillance** has become **non-negotiable**. These three elements must work **in unison**, forming a cohesive and ongoing program to safeguard critical business functions and information systems.

Governance, Risk, and Compliance (GRC) as a Service is no longer a luxury - it is a **strategic necessity**. It enables organizations to implement a **structured, standardized, and systematic** approach to managing business operations and their associated IT and OT environments.

The right GRC framework must be **tailored** based on:

- The **size** of the organization
- The **complexity** of its IT/OT infrastructure
- **Regulatory** and **industry-specific** compliance requirements

Importantly, GRC is not a one-time project. It is a **continuous journey** - one that evolves with technology, threats, and business demands. It should not be seen as a **cost center** or overhead, but rather as a **core management function**, embedded across the organizational ecosystem.

All industries - whether highly regulated or not - operate under some form of **standard or regulatory expectation**. While **scope and criteria may vary**, the **broad principles and structured approach to GRC remain universally applicable**.

In the upcoming chapters, we'll explore how organizations of **any size - from startups to large enterprises and SMEs** - can effectively **adopt, implement, and sustain** a practical GRC framework that aligns with their business objectives and security posture.

Chapter

2

Integrated and Unified GRC Implementation

1. Introduction

Governance, Risk, and Compliance (GRC), as introduced in earlier sections, is a **strategic enabler** that allows organizations to align their digital initiatives and IT-driven business processes with overall **business goals and objectives**. By adopting a **risk-based and structured approach**, organizations can effectively define, implement, and manage **information security policies and procedures** in accordance with **recognized best practices** and applicable **regional regulations and operational laws**.

With the **globalization of business operations** and the **dispersion of critical data** across on-premise data centers and multi-cloud environments, organizations are increasingly required to comply with **multiple information system security frameworks**. These include adherence to **regional cyber laws**, **industry-specific regulations**, and **global security standards**.

In this evolving landscape, the **traditional approach** of conducting IT and system audits using a **single security or audit framework** is becoming obsolete. It fails to effectively address the complex and overlapping compliance demands of today's hybrid environments.

To navigate this complexity, organizations must transition towards an **Integrated and Unified GRC Framework**, which enables better management of diverse **Information Security Management System (ISMS)** requirements.

This section explores:

- The **limitations of traditional GRC implementation models**
- The **advantages of adopting a managed GRC model**
- How **AI-enabled automation** can drive operational efficiency and accuracy in GRC functions

2. Concept of Integrated GRC framework

While **information system security requirements, standards, and regulations** may vary by **industry vertical** or **geographic location**, the **core information technology controls** often remain consistent in their objectives - i.e., to uphold **confidentiality, integrity, availability**, and **compliance**.

In the **Indian domestic market**, organizations may be subject to one or more of the following ISMS frameworks depending on their sector:

- ISO Standards such ISO27001, ISO22301, ISO27701, ISO42001, ISO/IEC 62243
- Regulator Cyber Security and Cyber Resiliency driven by RBI for Banks, SEBI for Securities Market, IRDAI for Insurance segment
- Custom regulations such as PCI_DSS, UPI guidelines , NBFC and others
- Data Privacy Laws/Act such as DPDPA
- Technology specific guidelines such and NIST, SOC 2

Given the overlap of requirements and the high cost of redundancy, organizations must implement an **integrated GRC model** that provides a **consolidated view of controls, risks, and compliance mandates**, while maintaining the **flexibility to adapt to various regulatory obligations**.

Likewise, similar **security standards and regulatory requirements** have been defined by global regulatory bodies and region-specific laws to govern information security, privacy, and compliance. These frameworks aim to ensure that organizations, regardless of their size or geography, adopt **consistent controls and risk management practices**.

The need for **harmonization of security controls and compliance requirements** has led to the evolution of integrated frameworks that can map and align controls across **multiple standards**. This integrated approach provides organizations with a **unified risk view**, reduces redundancy, and helps in managing audits more effectively.

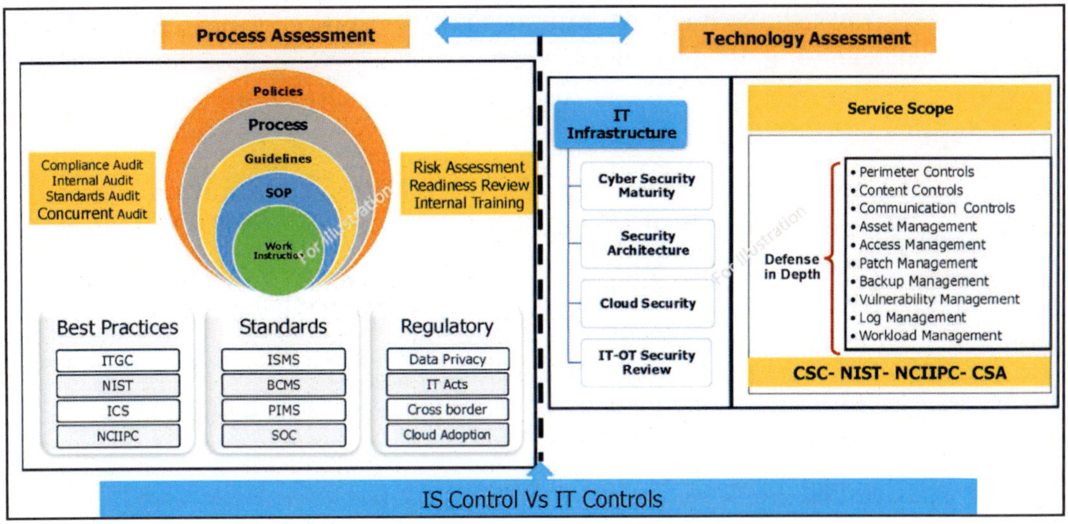

Figure 6 Integrated Framework Concept

GRC Implementation: Bridging Process and Technology Controls

Implementing a **GRC framework** involves aligning and integrating **Information System (IS) controls**, as identified during **process audits**, with corresponding **Information Technology (IT) controls**, as determined through **technology assessments**.

This alignment ensures a **holistic risk management approach,** where both **policy/ process-based governance** (left-hand side of Fig. 6) and **technology-driven controls** (right-hand side of Fig. 6) work in tandem to ensure compliance, risk mitigation, and security assurance.

The table below outlines various types of **GRC-related audits and assessments**, which may vary depending on the **industry vertical** and **regulatory requirements**:

Regulatory Compliance	Domestic(India) - RBI, SEBI, IRDA, NPCI, UIDAI, UPI, Cert-in, MOD, ISNP, NCIIPC, DOT, International – NESA, SAMA, MAS, HKMA, 22 CFR Part 11 and others
Standards Compliance	ISMS – ISO27001, PIMS – ISO27701, BCMS-22301, Quality -ISO9001, ITSM- ISO20000, OT – ISA/IEC 62443 and others
Framework Compliance	PCI – DSS, HIPAA, CMMC, C2M2, SAMA, COSO, SOC (1,2,3), NIST, CIS, FAIR, GDPR, DPDPA and others

The above list is **not exhaustive**, but it provides an overview of how the **scope of GRC is continuously evolving**. Each **industry vertical**, depending on the **complexity of its operations**, **regulatory exposure**, and **risk profile**, is increasingly adopting **one or more compliance frameworks**-often in parallel.

Although these regulations and standards are often **tailored to address regional or industry-specific requirements**, there is considerable **overlap** in the control objectives and implementation measures. This creates an opportunity to **streamline compliance** through an **integrated GRC audit approach**, reducing redundancy, audit fatigue, and operational overhead.

- **Universal Banking** where we need to comply to standards , multiple regulations and frameworks
- **ITES Operations** where we need to comply with different standards and frameworks to address client delivery requirement
- **Pharma** clients, need to comply with ISO, HIPAA and FDA regulations
- **Utilities sector** such as power, water, Oil, needs compliance against NIST, ISO for its IT and OT environment
- **Cloud provider** needs compliance against majority of the standards, regulations

This is where the **implementation of an Integrated GRC approach** proves highly beneficial. It not only aligns multiple compliance requirement but also enables organizations to manage risk holistically and efficiently across various domains.

In the **subsequent section**, we will delve into a **comparative analysis of the traditional GRC approach versus modern AI-enabled, tool-driven GRC implementations**. This will highlight the advantages and limitations of each model and provide insights into how technology can significantly enhance GRC outcomes.

3. Traditional GRC Audit and Assessment Approach

Historically, **Governance, Risk, and Compliance (GRC) Audits and Assessments** have been conducted using a **manual, checklist-driven methodology**. This approach relies heavily on established standards, regulatory requirements, or industry-specific frameworks. For each audit or assessment engagement, a control-based checklist is used as the primary tool to verify whether controls are:

Applicable to the organization's environment

Implemented in accordance with the defined requirements

Operating effectively in practice

While this traditional method / approach ensures basic compliance and provides traceable documentation, it is often limited in scalability, contextual analysis, and adaptability-especially in hybrid, multi-framework environments.

Below is a **sample template of a traditional GRC checklist** used during such assessments:

Policy Standard Statement	Reponsibility Matrix				Standard 1	Standard 2	Standard 3	Applicability
	R	A	C	I	ISO27001 :2022	IS 42001	NIST	

Documentation Level	Implementation Level	Automation level	Auditors Comment	Organisation Comments / Additional inputs	Maturity Rating

Figure 7 GRC Assessment checklist for illustration only

The definition of the columns as per table are presented below for easy of understanding

- **Policy standard -** it is the control objective as defined in policy statement. It can be considered as domain with the policy document such as Asset Management domain, access management domain and others
- **Policy standard statement-** it is the control as defined in the control objectives. Each domain will have multiple controls e.g. within Asset management – asset definition, asset nomenclature, asset location are types of control and others
- **Responsibility matrix -** defines who is owner, who is accountable, who is to be consulted and who all to be kept informed to have a proper governance
- **Applicability -** it defines whether the control is applicable for the organization and whether organization is wanting to look for some deviations as required

- **Documentation Level, Implementation level, automation –** it defines the current status of deployment of the controls and control objectives
- **Operative effectiveness –** it is measure to evaluate if the control is followed as per defined policies
- **Maturity rating -** it is defined based on the weighted percentage
- Auditors' comment and organizational comments are feedback and response based on the audit findings, which can be considered as gaps in the current posture and a room for improvement as part of continuous service improvement
- Each column further can have a data validation field defined, for easy of population of the sheet and for building a standardization within the audit team. Validation can be color coded to provide a more visual exchange

Important Note on Checklist Customization

The **checklist provided earlier is a sample template** intended to illustrate the thought process behind building a GRC audit checklist. This template must be **customized and contextualized** to suit the unique requirements of an organization.

Customization should be driven by:

- The **industry vertical** of the organization
- The **applicable regulatory and compliance frameworks**
- The **complexity and maturity** of the IT and business environment
- The **geographic or jurisdictional applicability** of standards or laws

Each audit engagement requires a **fit-for-purpose checklist** to ensure accurate, relevant, and actionable outcomes.

The traditional approach has been very effective and extremely useful when doing a point in time audit or doing an audit against a single framework. But in today's scenario organizations are subjected to multiple audits, each by different auditors, thus manual checklist-based audit has certain inherent shortcoming. The likely short comings of traditional audit are:

- Multiple sheets, multiple templates to be maintained
- Each template will need an initial manual effort and mapping with respect to controls and control objectives

- Decentralized templates and risk registers making the accessibility difficult and chances of overlooking some of the controls
- Difficult to consolidate multiple risk reports, excel sheets etc.
- Regulators who require continuous monitoring, which is very difficult with manual processes
- Multiple audits are to be done based on multiple regulatory audits and compliance requirement
- Teams working in silos resulting in inefficient information exchange and opaque accountability management
- Non-Unified method of multiple auditors
- Absence of Integrated audit framework
- Difficult to maintain trending, reporting and dashboarding
- Varied third parties / vendors in the eco system resulting in different vendor risk assessment requirements
- Technology disruption and the wide spread use of various technical assets with the combination of legacy and current technology
- Auditor- Auditee co-ordination is challenging due to multiple sheets and formats

4. GRC Automated Tool based Audit and Assessment Approach

To overcome the current **inherent limitations of traditional checklist-driven audits**, organizations are increasingly adopting **next-generation, AI-enabled GRC audit platforms**. These platforms offer an **automated, intelligent, and integrated** approach to Governance, Risk, and Compliance management.

With the growing complexity of compliance mandates, evolving threat landscapes, and the need for continuous assurance, automation is no longer a luxury-it is a necessity.

- Various tools and platform are now available to help conduct these audits in a structured workflow driven approach
- Platforms provided by different OEM are available to be deployed either onsite or also offered as a SaaS platform deployed on cloud

- Based on the data localization, data security and privacy needs organization can thus consider deploying available options
- Many platforms have a modular approach towards addressing different areas of GRC i.e. modules for compliance assessment, modules for vendors risk assessment, modules for operational risk assessment and others
- Platforms further also have the capability to be integrated with deployed IT tools to enhance the automation and build more operational efficiency

Leveraging the capabilities of modern GRC automation platforms, combined with professional expertise, enables organizations to gain several advantages over traditional, manual, checklist-based methods. The key benefits include:

- Easier Compliance & Control Audit & Assessment
- Better employee risk awareness & engagement
- Compliance workflow enables to improvise strategic planning and decision making
- Online availability of risk registers, provide better visibility
- Build efficiency and optimization of professional time
- Ability to track end to end issues
- Single platform for management and cross functional workflow automation
- Effortless compliance mapping with inbuilt intelligence through AI technologies
- Multiple standards and regulations can be audited in a single go
- Standardization of policies, process and audit methodologies
- Reduction on audit fatigue
- Better control and transparency between auditor and auditee
- Inbuilt reporting and dashboarding options providing flexibility and ease of reporting, and tracking KPI/KRA
- Reduced dependencies of skills and professionals

A typical step to gap assessment audit approach for any type of Information Security Management System includes:

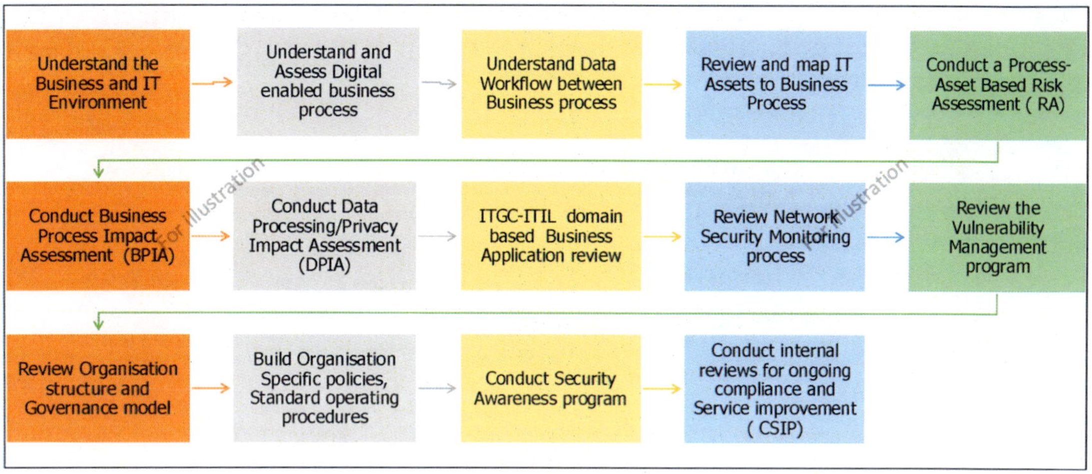

Figure 8 Audit Workflow

When an audit is carried out using a traditional, manual methodology-whether sequentially or in parallel-the following are the **standard deliverables** typically expected from the engagement:

- Project plan
- Fresh / upgraded polices
- BPIA report for select applications
- DPIA report from select business processes
- ITGC based review of Applications
- Checklist based gap assessment report
- Data flow diagrams
- Templates of stand operating process
- VM calendar
- BCP/ITDR review

5. GRC Automation Implementation Approach

Considering the overall requirement of **adhering to compliance obligations**, **managing information and operational risks**, and ensuring that the process is **system-driven and governance-enabled**, organizations should move towards adopting **"GRC as a Service (GRCaaS)"** as a part of their organizational culture.

GRC automation should no longer be seen as a standalone or occasional exercise but rather as an **embedded, ongoing, and scalable program**-interlinked with business operations, security governance, and enterprise risk management.

The figure depicted below provides a **snapshot of the GRC automation objectives**, and how automation aligns the **strategic, tactical, and operational** layers of governance, risk, and compliance.

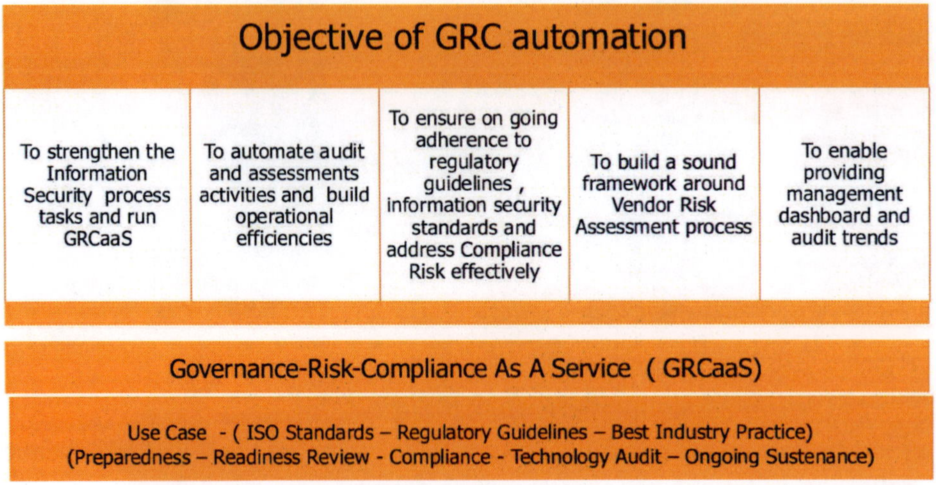

Figure 9 GRC Automation Benefits – A View point

While evaluating the deployment of automation in GRC, it is important to select a platform based on certain critical criteria to ensure it meets organizational needs and supports effective governance, risk, and compliance management. The key factors to consider include:

- How many standards, regulations or guidelines to be supported in parallel
- Are the tools only used for Information security governance or other operational governance
- How many audits and assessment are being planned for the period i.e. audit frequency or audit calendar per year
- Is it for single organization or for a group (hub and spoke model)
- Are you wanting to have on-premise or on SaaS platform (based on data localization requirement)
- What are the GRC modules required as mandatory (asset management, risk register, vendor risk management, reporting, compliance mapping, policy build etc.)
- Is integration of current tools required i.e. integration of VM tools, IAM tools, Security monitoring tools etc.

- Do you require usage of AI platform (for mapping, for threat modelling, for threat intelligence, for asset inventory etc.)
- How many audit roles and how many auditee roles required
- What reporting dashboard and reports is the expectation

A typical workflow of a GRC automation tools is shown below:

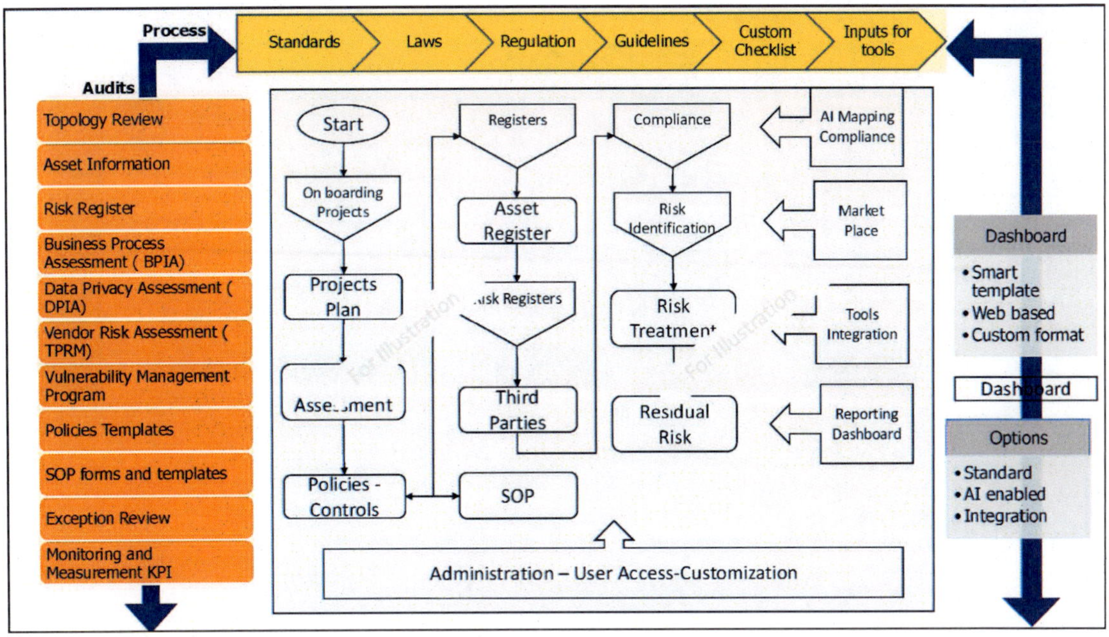

Figure 10 GRC Platform Logical View for Illustration

The model workflow can be considered running in matrix model

- The top bar running horizontally addressing the organisation requirements considering various standards, laws , regulations (Many tools have inbuilt market place through which the latest versions are readily available and can be merged with the audit requirement).
- The left-hand side running vertically, has the different risk assessment modules which can operate individually in standalone mode or in integrated embedded model.
- The centre is the workflow which represent the overall operational method of matrix model including integration with external tools and AI models.
- The right-hand side presents management reporting and dashboarding view point

The above schematic gives a technical view point of the implementation of the model. The same when presented from management perspective can be viewed as a layered approach running vertically across all organisational business functions, and surrounded with a tight GRC framework aligned with best industry standard practices.

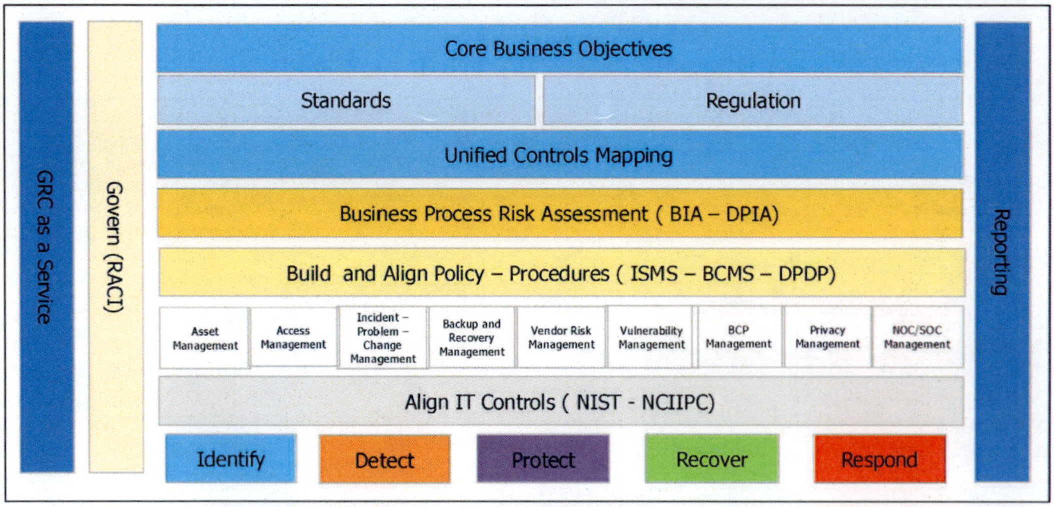

Figure 11 GRC Framework 3Dimensional View

6. Conclusion

The choice between traditional and tool-based GRC audit approaches largely depends on the complexity and scale of the organizational environment. Regardless of the method, adopting an **integrated audit and assessment approach** is essential to enhance operational efficiency, minimize duplication of efforts, and reduce audit fatigue for both auditors and auditees.

A well-designed GRC tool should provide clear and concise summaries of audit findings, enabling stakeholders and information security teams to effectively prioritize remediation actions and resource allocation.

In the subsequent sections, we will take a deep dive into each of these modules, providing detailed insights to better understand the GRC requirements across various domains, thereby enabling organizations to tailor their governance, risk, and compliance efforts effectively.

Chapter

3

GRC in IT Asset and Inventory Management

1. Introduction

The scale and complexity of Information Technology (IT) infrastructure in organizations-be it small, medium, or large-continue to grow steadily. IT assets include physical hardware, software licenses, and virtual / cloud-based resources. These assets can be categorized into end-user devices, data center hardware, and cloud assets. Moreover, with the rise of remote working and mobile devices, IT assets often operate in geographically distributed and dynamic environments.

Effective governance of IT assets requires tracking their usage, monitoring physical and virtual locations, optimizing license utilization, and ensuring timely updates such as software patches and firmware upgrades. As a key component of Governance, Risk, and Compliance (GRC) implementation, robust IT Asset and Inventory Management is foundational to mitigating associated risks and ensuring compliance with organizational policies and regulatory guidelines.

2. IT Asset Management (ITAM) Basics

IT Asset Management (ITAM) involves the comprehensive tracking and management of IT assets throughout their entire lifecycle-from procurement and deployment to usage, maintenance, and eventual disposal. Different organizational teams rely on ITAM data for diverse purposes:

- **IT Operations:** For asset usage tracking, maintenance, and software patch management
- **Procurement:** To manage purchasing and vendor relationships
- **Finance:** To monitor asset costs, depreciation, and budget planning

An effective ITAM framework enables the organization to maintain control over its IT environment, minimize operational risks, and improve cost efficiency by ensuring assets are properly utilized and governed.

Implementing ITAM across an enterprise helps to:

- Managing asset lifecycle
- Support in adhering to compliance
- Enable optimal usage of resources thereby by having a control on expenses
- Support in projecting addon requirements

ITAM thus serves as a prime function in building the GRC framework of any organization, as assets form the backbone of the digital infrastructure. Hence, implementing a robust structure covering all Information Technology assets is critical. Across all standards and regulations, IT Asset Management is recognized as one of the primary governance functions that organizations must define and maintain.

ITAM in a Nutshell in today's environment comprises the following key elements:

- **HAM (Hardware Asset Management)** - Desktops, Laptops, Servers, Network Switches, Routers, Security appliance, CCTV and others
- **SAM (Software Asset Management)** - OEM driven Operating system software, application software, Data base software, middleware and others
- **CAM (Cloud Asset Management)** - Native cloud workloads, Cloud VM and others

The following outlines the overall objectives, positioning, and scope of IT Asset Management (ITAM) as defined within the **ITIL (Information Technology Infrastructure Library)** framework:

Objective

- Provide a view of IT assets enabling organizations to identify asset location , understand the usage requirements and assess potential OEM / Vendor License compliance risk

ITAM

- Information Technology Infrastructure Library (ITIL) describes ITAM as "all of the infrastructure and processes necessary for the effective management, control and protection of hardware and software IT assets within an organization, throughout all stages of its lifecycle

Scope

- Deals with Assessment and Review of IT Assets with organizational physical , contractual , and financial requirement wrt Inventory , Usage , Compliance , Maintenance and Vendor Support , and procurement and budget

Figure 12 ITAM Overview

3. ITAM and GRC

IT assets form the fundamental resources that power an organization's digital business processes. All binary information flows through these assets, whether hardware, software, or cloud infrastructure. Therefore, ensuring **availability** of these assets is critical being one of the core principles in the CIA triad of security (Confidentiality, Integrity, Availability).

Failure in any hardware or software component can lead to non-availability of critical business data, directly impacting business operations. Similarly, hardware failures such as disk or memory corruption can compromise the **integrity** of data, another vital element of the security triad.

To guarantee that digital data transacted across IT assets (including hardware, software, applications, and databases) remains **available** and **integrity-protected** at all times, organizations must identify and mitigate risks effectively. This ensures the IT infrastructure operates optimally and reliably.

Moreover, maintaining IT assets-along with their licenses and subscriptions-in alignment with operational and functional business requirements ensures compliance across various regulatory and internal policies.

Since IT asset management involves multiple departments responsible for procurement, maintenance, monitoring, and support, establishing a **well-defined governance framework** around IT Asset and Inventory Management is essential.

Adopting a GRC framework thus helps build a structured and transparent approach for implementing IT Asset and Inventory Management policies. This, in turn, enhances operational effectiveness and fosters resilience in managing IT assets.

4. ITAM Implementation and Deployment Approach

ITAM is leveraged across various departments within an organization to manage the entire asset lifecycle. Some typical use cases include:

For IT departments or by Infosec team

- Track the usage of deployment IT assets while it is in used by professionals
- Tracking the operational factors with respect to its availability, rightful usage and in compliance with usage policies
- Track hardware assets for its availability and functionality, software assets from licensing perspective, maintenance and support perspective from OEM, patching and upgrades of assets from security and bug fixing and others

For Procurement department

- Track the usage for assets from ownership to disposal
- Track asset label, expiry of usage of product and services for various OEM assets with respect expiry terms of usage, for providing information for budgeting the requirements of annual maintenance support

For Finance department

- Providing budgeting for financial expenses
- For calculation information on cost depression and other factors impacting the financial balance sheet

ITAM Deployment Approaches

IT Asset and Inventory Management (ITAM) can be implemented in multiple ways within an organization, depending on its size, asset volume, and operational requirements. Common deployment models include:

- **Automated Asset and Inventory Tools:** These platforms provide real-time tracking, monitoring, and reporting of IT assets with minimal manual intervention
- **Configuration Management Database (CMDB) Model:** This approach integrates asset information into a centralized database that maps relationships and dependencies between IT components, often used in IT Service Management (ITSM)

- **Traditional Manual Worksheets:** In smaller or less complex environments, ITAM may be managed using spreadsheets or manual records

The choice of deployment depends on factors such as:

- Organization size and asset complexity
- Centralized versus distributed asset management needs
- Compliance requirements with applicable standards and regulations
- Overall business impact, operational efficiency, and resource availability

While no specific standard or regulation mandates the exact ITAM implementation methodology, guidelines exist to help organizations adopt a suitable framework. This allows ITAM deployments to range from manual, semi-automated, to fully automated, based on organizational maturity and needs.

The following schematic illustrates how an asset management platform adds value to an organization's GRC framework, aligning with the NIST Cybersecurity Framework functions:

Identify → Detect → Prevent → Respond → Recover → Govern

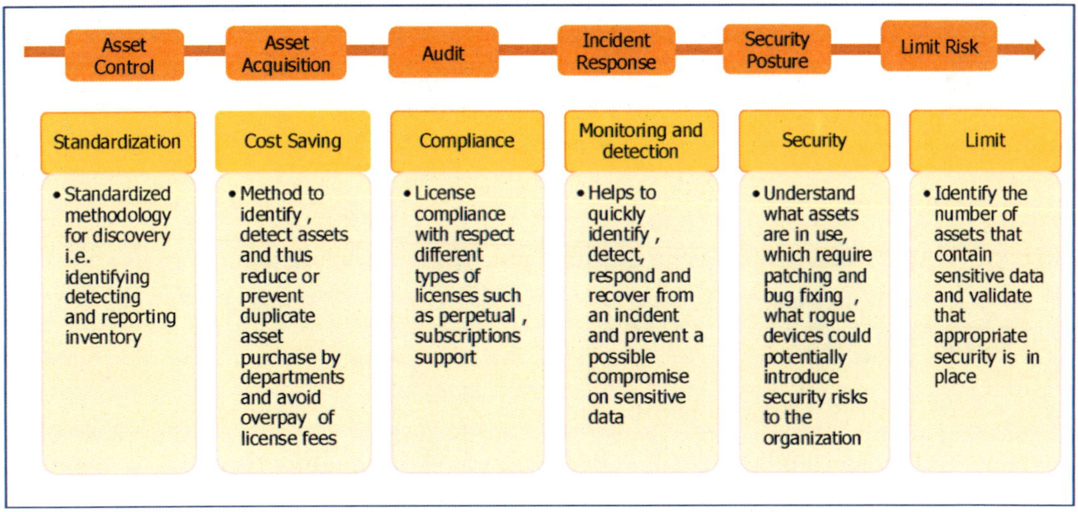

Figure 13 ITAM and NIST

Often, organizations use the term **Asset Management** interchangeably, but it is important to distinguish between **IT Asset Management (ITAM)** and **Configuration Management Database (CMDB)**.

ITAM is a more technical discipline focused on tracking and managing IT assets throughout their lifecycle - including hardware, software, and virtual/cloud assets.

CMDB, on the other hand, is a centralized repository that documents the state and posture of various IT assets, known as **Configuration Items (CIs)**. The CMDB not only records these assets, but also captures their relationships and interdependencies across departments and business functions. This interconnected view helps forecast the impact of changes, supports IT service stability, and is primarily leveraged in **IT Service Management (ITSM)**.

While the CMDB approach and methodology are critical, they are not covered in detail in this section. However, some aspects related to CMDB are discussed in the **Business Process-driven Approach** section.

5. Practical ITAM Policy Sample

Objective: Maintain an accurate, up-to-date inventory of IT assets to ensure their identification, classification, and security, aligning with regulatory requirements and best practices.

1.1 Scope Coverage

- **Physical Assets**: Servers, desktops, laptops, networking equipment, storage devices, IT and IoT devices
- **Software Assets**: Licensed applications, operating systems, and development tools
- **Virtual Assets**: Virtual machines, cloud infrastructure, containers, and virtual desk tops
- **Data Assets**: Databases, file repositories, and backup systems
- **Peripheral Devices**: Printers, scanners, and other connected devices

1.2 Policy Statements

1.2.1 Centralized IT Asset Repository

- Implement and maintain a **centralized IT asset inventory** using a robust asset management tool.
- Ensure the repository captures critical details, including asset name, type, serial number, make ,model, location , ownership, configuration details, end of life (EOL) / end of support (EOS)

1.2.2 Asset Classification

- Classify assets based on their criticality and sensitivity into critical , non-critical
- Use classification to prioritize security controls, monitoring, and incident response efforts.

1.2.3 Asset Onboarding and Decommissioning

- Define a standard process for onboarding new assets, ensuring they are documented in the inventory system.
- Configured with baseline security measures before deployment.
- Establish secure decommissioning procedures, secure erasure or destruction of data
- Removal from the active inventory
- Recycling or disposal per environmental regulations

1.2.4 Inventory Accuracy and Audits

- Conduct periodic inventory audits (quarterly or semi-annually) to ensure the accuracy of the IT asset repository
- Reconcile discrepancies, including: Missing, duplicated, or unregistered assets. Updated asset ownership or location changes
- Maintain audit logs and reports for compliance and accountability

1.2.5. Asset Risk Assessment

- Perform regular risk assessments for critical assets to identify vulnerabilities and potential impacts
- Update risk profiles based on evolving threats, asset changes, or operational dependencies

1.2.6 Access and Ownership

- Assign ownership for each asset, ensuring clear accountability for, maintenance and updates, monitoring security controls and compliance with organizational policies.

Roles and Responsibilities for e.g.

- IT Asset Management Team
- Department Heads
- Employees
- Internal Audit Team

1.2.7 Deviation

- Any exclusion to this policy can be mentioned

Note: The above policy has been purpose built for this document to highlight possible areas which can be covered and incorporated. Controls and control objectives can be considered based on applicability and its implementation requirements. Please note the template has been given for reference purpose only. It will need to be customised, modified to meet individual organisation requirement.

6. ITAM Standard Operating Procedure – Template

A Standard Operating Procedure (SOP) can take the form of either a working document or a worksheet that defines the methods and processes for gathering and populating information relevant to the scope of the requirement.

- From a general perspective, an SOP is a **procedure document-**a written explanation of how and what to do
- From a technical perspective, it can also be a **worksheet-driven tool-**a practical guide to help execute the process

When developing ITAM requirements, whether manual or automated, it is essential to focus on the overall objectives and functional usage, and to clearly define the success criteria and key steps.

- First step is to build a matrix table identifying all areas of information that needs to be gathered, mapped and reported, to get a holistic view of the profile, posture and associated risk
- Second step is to determine what needs to be discovered through automated tools and what can be done using manual method
- Third step is evaluating options for tools / CMDB as per business size
- Explore integration with organization ERP or other IT tools as applicable
- Consider utilization of Managed GRC platform

The overall initial approach towards asset information collection is shown in the figures for illustration

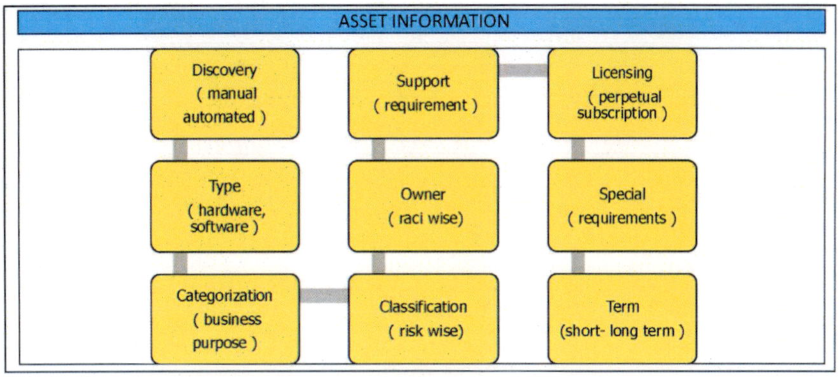

Figure 14 ITAM Discovery workflow

To help the above sample template of typical SOP has been shown which can be used as starting point

- **End Point Asset Inventory**

Sr	Location	Name	Date	Last User	Last User: Admin Privileges	Asset Type	Domain	IP Address	MAC Address	MFG	Model	Serial Number
Serial Number	BIOS/Firmware	Processor	RAM (MB)	Hard Drive Model	Hard Drive Type	OS	OS Build Version	OS End of Life (Y/N)	OS End of Service (Y/N)	End Point Security	Group Policy	End point Encryption

- **Application Asset Inventory**

SN	Business Application Name	Custom / Home grown / COTS	Used for	Developed by	Maintained by	Business owners	Deployed on how many Servers	Which Users have access	What is the method of Access	IP / Domain	Internet IP	Extranet IP
SN	How frequent change happen	VAPT testing	ITGC Audit	User roles Mgmt	Acesss Mgmt	Encryption	Log Mgmt	Data backup	Network monitoring	Change Mgmt	Incident Mgmt	Compliance if any

- **Network Security Asset Inventory**

Sn	Device Location	Asset Type	Make/ Manufacturer	Model	Serial Number	OS/Firmware	EOL/ EOS	Remark	AMC Status	Warranty Status	Auditing enabled

Figure 15 Asset Inventory Templates

The above tables gives an indicative approach to gathering information and is not comprehensive.

- Organisation based on the complexity and flexibility can consider changes to suit its requirements
- Few parameters can be captured through tools; few can be added manually
- The frequency of monitoring parameters can be defined based on organizational needs-such as continuous, daily, weekly, or monthly-to maintain a live, running log that supports trend analysis and measurement of operational effectiveness.
- Based on operating mode - reporting , dashboarding mechanism can be defined which can provide different perspective of IT Assets
- We can either define asset-based risk assessment or we can map asset to business process and do a process-based risk assessment (being discussed in next section)

7. Conclusion

IT Asset Management (ITAM) and Governance, Risk, and Compliance (GRC) are intrinsically linked in addressing the Confidentiality, Integrity, and Availability (CIA) triad of Information Security. Without a structured ITAM framework, the availability of critical resources can be compromised, resulting in significant disruptions to business functions.

The risks associated with IT assets can be effectively mapped to business processes, providing a comprehensive foundation for conducting Business Impact Analysis (BIA), which will be explored in subsequent sections.

A holistic ITAM program-covering Hardware Asset Management (HAM), Software Asset Management (SAM), and Cloud Asset Management (CAM)-should be a core component of any Information Security Management System (ISMS) when building an integrated GRC framework.

In the next section, we will delve deeper into different types and methods of Risk Assessment, along with the recommended approaches for effective Risk Management.

Chapter

4

GRC and Risk Management

1. Introduction

To ensure the **Confidentiality, Integrity, Availability (CIA),** and **Privacy** of sensitive organizational data, it is essential to identify and detect associated risks and threats within the digital infrastructure. These risks originate from both **insiders** and **outsiders** within the operational business environment. Preventing potential attacks that could disrupt IT systems and business operations, requires a well-defined **Risk Assessment (RA) and Management program** that operates at the core of the organization's Information System Security Governance framework.

Risks associated with IT can arise from technological implementation gaps, non-compliance with regulatory requirements, or operational deficiencies. Beyond IT and cybersecurity risks, organizations also face other types of risks including financial, market, investment, and credit risks.

For the purpose of this discussion, the focus will be limited to **Cyber Risk** associated with digital IT and business infrastructure, which may lead to **data loss, digital fraud,** and **reputational damage** to the organization's brand.

2. Risk Assessment Methodologies

In today's world, IT is indispensable to business functions. Nearly all business processes are increasingly automated through next-generation AI platforms. As cyber-attacks and threats continue to rise-and as assets spread across on-premises and multiple cloud environments-organizations' IT infrastructure is exposed to risks from both internal and external sources.

Some risks are more significant than others, and mitigation costs can vary widely. Therefore, it is critical to proactively identify and assess risk areas and to implement a **formalized risk assessment process** to prioritize and address these risks efficiently.

Multiple Risk Assessment methodologies exist, each with its own focus and approach. The following section briefly reviews these methods to provide an overview and help organizations choose the most appropriate approach based on their environment and risk appetite:

Asset Based Risk Assessment :

Traditional organization have been doing asset-based risk assessment. Every IT asset hardware, software, networks, cloud and others are reviewed with respective to its criticality, exposure to likely threats and associated risk to IT environment.

This asset based has been centered around the IT assets / IT department and possibly looked in silos. This possible fall short of the business process view. For e.g. a Firewall risks and controls are easy to understand at individual asset level, but the same is going to have an impact on other business process.

Process Based Risk Assessment :

While Asset based risk assessment gives a vertical view considering asset as priority, Process based assessment helps to scan risks across the horizontal digital business functions and departments, and thus enable to map business applications with IT Assets.

This method of mapping one business application to many assets, or many applications to some unique IT assets , helps to give a business process perspective to the business owners. This can help to prioritize criticality at process level (application level), while the same priority can be rolled to associated IT assets.

Quantitative Based Risk Assessment: It is mostly a combination of asset or process based with addition of financial value derived by statistical method and techniques, to assign a numerical value or weightage to risks, based on which financial impact is arrived. This may help in providing a more objective and quantifiable understand of risk.

The result based on this approach is sometimes too complex and may not be understood beyond the board rooms or difficult for IT team to understand and corelate.

Using Risk Quantification model such as FAIR (Factor Analysis of Information Risk), VaR(Value at Risk) and integrating the same with AI, there are many OEM tools which can do this type of risk assessment.

Other Based Risk Assessment :

Another method which is a combination of Asset based Risk Assessment and Vulnerability based Risk Assessment. Here post doing VA of the assets, its criticality is determined. This provides an effective assessment for new vulnerabilities, but beyond that it is not able to prove to be effective.

An alternative to Vulnerability based RA there is Threat based Risk Assessment. By conducting exercises, such as social engineering, red teaming, cyber drill testing, organization's review the Threat posture and arrive at a model.

Summary of Risk Assessment Methodologies

Each Risk Assessment methodology has its own strengths and limitations. Choosing the right approach depends on the organization's overall business needs and the type of outputs desired from the assessment.

- **Quantitative Methods** are often preferred by board members and senior stakeholders as they provide measurable, financial-impact-focused data that can guide investment and risk appetite decisions
- **Asset-based or Process-based Assessments** tend to align naturally with IT organizations. These methods are typically easier to understand, implement, and communicate across technical teams
- **Threat-based and Vulnerability Assessment (VA) based** methods may be suitable for small enterprises with limited environments, but they often encounter limitations in large organizations due to the breadth of testing scenarios required

In the following subsection, we introduce a model that can be viewed either as asset-based or process-based, offering flexibility depending on organizational context and maturity.

3. Risk Assessment / Management Approach

The purpose of this procedure is to establish a **structured approach** for identifying, assessing, and mitigating risks related to business and support processes. The ultimate goal is to minimize the impact of threats and vulnerabilities, while ensuring compliance with applicable standards and regulations.

This procedure applies across all business and support functions within the organization, including IT, operations, finance, and human resources. It encompasses the entire risk lifecycle: **risk identification, risk assessment, risk treatment, and continuous risk monitoring.**

The following workflow diagrams illustrate a practical approach to building a **Risk Register** and implementing a comprehensive **Risk Assessment process** tailored to organizational needs.

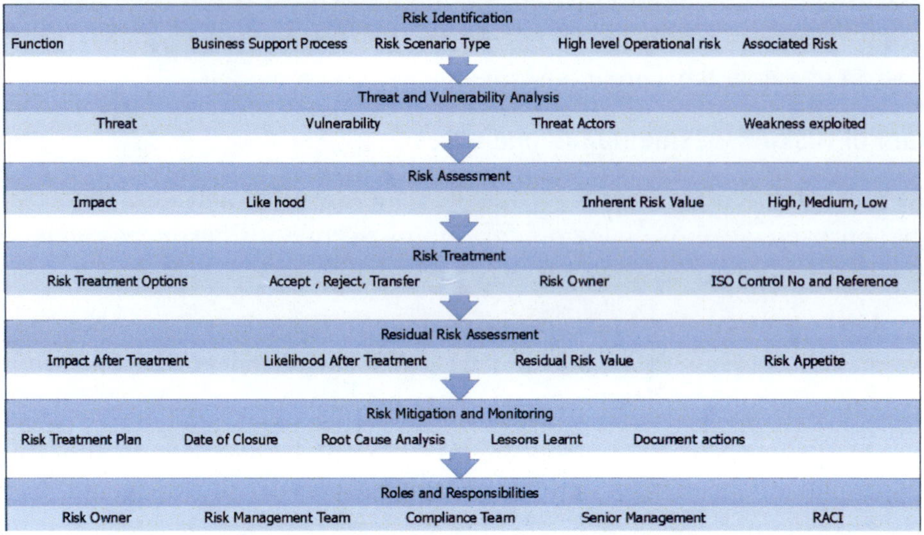

Figure 16 Risk Assessment Framework

The upper row of rectangular squares illustrates the sequential flow of activities involved in the Risk Assessment approach. These steps represent the key phases that guide the process from start to finish.

The lower row of squares provides detailed guidance on how the risk assessment plan and overall approach should be defined. It outlines the critical parameters and considerations necessary when building the risk management framework. This includes defining scope, identifying risk criteria, establishing roles and responsibilities, and determining assessment techniques - all essential elements to ensure a robust and tailored risk assessment process.

4. Deliverables out of Risk Assessment Approach indicative

1. Risk Register template

- Risk register document or worksheet can act as a risk management tool which can be populated with the above defined approach to meet the respective needs of business
- The tool can be flexible enough to either provide a process-based view or asset-based view as per the defined GRC framework of the organization
- The register will have all information of threats, risks, impact, likelihood, criticality, residual risk and others

- Many standards do recommend adoption of process driven framework which can further be used to address other areas of GRC such as Business Continuity Planning, IT disaster recovery, Data Privacy and Protection and others

2. Root Cause Analysis template

- Details of the incident covering all information of how, what when with respect incident
- Details of the root cause of occurrence as found after analysis
- Details of lessons learnt and what action plan has taken to prevent reoccurrence

3. Risk Appetite

- Risk Appetite By definition IT Risk Appetite (ITRA) is the amount of risk that organisation is prepared to accept, tolerate, or be exposed to at any point in time. Alternately the overall impact to business functions, an organization is ready to accept on a board level
- Residual Risk Assessment is used to determine whether risk is accepted, transferred , or migrated which may lead to actual Risk Appetite

Risk Appetite Methodology

A well-defined risk appetite forces a company to include the risk factor in any major strategic or tactical decision and it is an iterative process. At a broad level while adapting to an IT Risk Appetite (ITRA) statement which is cornerstone of risk management, the following approach should be considered:

- Develop a mandate and framework from Senior Management, Board representative
- Understand Organisation's strategy ,its risk profile and identify Risk Appetite of Stakeholders (internal and external) and the expectations
- Develop a metrics to rate and map risk across different risk types (financial, non-financial) as per the impact
- Develop ITRA Governance mechanism, accountability and report
- Define tolerance, limits and targets for each identified risk area
- Define process for periodic monitoring, measurement and reconciliation of risk profile to Risk Appetite
- Onboard approval of the statement

5. Conclusion

Risk Assessment and Risk Management are two sides of the same coin. Risk Assessment focuses on identifying and defining the risks as part of the GRC program, while Risk Management addresses the application and ongoing maintenance of risk mitigation measures. The risk register acts as a living document, continuously maintained, monitored, and reviewed to reflect the current risk posture.

Organizations have the flexibility to customize risk criteria and factors according to their specific business needs and risk appetite. As part of a Managed GRC approach, organizations can integrate Cyber Risk Assessment with Operational Risk Assessment to develop an unified and comprehensive risk management framework, that aligns with the organizational structure and business objectives.

Chapter

5

GRC and Business Process Impact Assessment

1. Introduction

In the previous sections, we covered the foundational GRC elements related to IT Asset Management and Risk Assessment. We explored various methodologies and approaches to conducting risk assessments on IT infrastructure and its associated business processes. Business process mapping provides a comprehensive walkthrough of the entire process flow and data flow across business applications. This, in turn, helps identify the IT assets and business units involved at each stage.

Reviewing application architecture and data flow delivers valuable insights into the criticality of applications from the perspective of people, processes, and technology, as well as their alignment with business objectives. This perspective allows organizations to understand which applications, if unavailable, could have significant operational, financial, or business impact.

The analysis conducted at this level is known as **Business Impact Analysis (BIA)** or **Business Process Impact Analysis (BPIA)**.

2. BIA in depth

Business Impact Analysis (BIA) forms a core component of the **Business Continuity Management System (BCMS)** as defined by ISO 22301. BCMS establishes a structured framework for organizations to assess, review, implement, manage, and continuously improve processes that protect against disruptive incidents, reduce their likelihood, and ensure effective recovery.

Disruptions may arise from IT asset failures, connectivity issues between locations, or natural disasters (e.g., earthquakes, lightning, power outages) which can cause loss of accessibility to critical operational data and its business operations. These scenarios are addressed within an organization's IT Disaster Recovery Plan, where BIA plays a crucial role.

The key objectives of a BIA include:

- Review business process to evaluate and estimate the financial loss / impacts for each business unit considering worst case scenarios
- Review, evaluate and estimate operational impacts for each business unit, considering worst case scenarios
- Identify the organization's business unit processes and the estimated recovery time frame for each business unit

The rest of this chapter focuses on how to conduct a comprehensive Business Impact Analysis (BIA) for various identified critical digital business processes. The BIA serves as a cornerstone for understanding the potential impact of disruptions on the enterprise and forms the basis for effective continuity and recovery planning.

The schematic representation below provides a high-level overview of the BIA process, illustrating the key stages involved in identifying critical business functions, analyzing their dependencies and impacts, and implementing a robust BIA program aligned with organizational objectives and risk appetite.

This approach ensures that organizations, can systematically assess vulnerabilities, prioritize the recovery efforts, and thus maintain resilience against both anticipated and unforeseen disruptions.

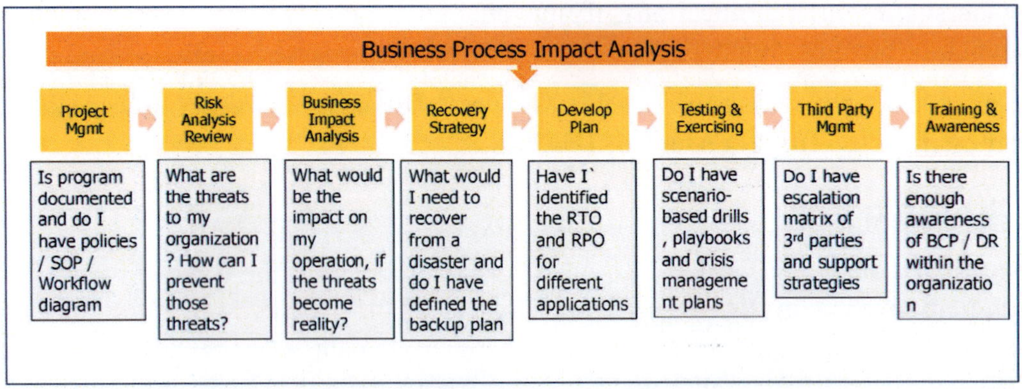

Figure 17 Business Impact Analysis High Level View

3. BIA methodology

Conducting a Business Impact Analysis (BIA) might sound like a heavy-lifting task-and honestly, it is-but it's one of the most valuable exercises an organization can undertake to stay resilient in the face of disruption.

Whether it's an IT system crash, a cyberattack, or something as unpredictable as a natural disaster, understanding how these incidents impact your critical business processes is key. That's where BIA steps in. When done right, it doesn't just give you a list of "what's important"-it helps you prioritize resources, streamline recovery, and build serious confidence across your teams.

But here's the catch: **BIA isn't just a job for IT**. It's a collaborative effort that brings together tech teams, operations, HR, finance, and all those behind-the-scenes heroes who keep the business running. The stronger your cross-functional collaboration between teams, the more meaningful your results will be.

Here's a **practical, phased approach** to make your BIA initiative not just doable, but successful:

- **Identify Critical Business Functions :**
    - Which business processes are running in the environment
    - Which digital applications are associated
    - Which IT assets are supporting the digital application
    - Which all Departments are involved
    - Which all OEM / Vendors need to be considered
- **Review and Assess Severity of Impact**
    - What is the consequence of any non-availability with respect to business operations
    - What are the consequences with respect to legal and contractual requirements
    - Is it a contractual level which needs to be adhered
    - Are there any penalties associated with the service levels
    - Is it an internal impact or external impact
    - What are the tangible financial cost associated with a down time
- **Define Recovery Strategies**
    - Define the Recovery Time Objective (RTO)
    - Define the Recovery Point Objective (RPO)
    - Align backup requirement

- **Document the BIA and BCP plan**
  - o Discuss BCP needs from people, process, technology
  - o Use realistic scenarios, Review requirements of cyber drill exercise as required
  - o Document the plan
  - o Define roles and responsibility matrix
- **BCP Training Develop critical skills**
  - o Are employees assigned to recovery strategies, across various departments trained fully on the process and methodology
  - o Are employees aware of the overall BCP and BIA and familiar with all aspects

Organizations typically kick off their BIA exercises using a **questionnaire or checklist-based approach** to collect detailed input from various departments. This helps in understanding how different business process functions, what systems they rely on, and what kind of impact a disruption could cause. It's a practical, scalable way to gather insights across the enterprise without overwhelming teams.

Below is a **template snapshot** that can help you get started. The columns are just **indicative**, and you're encouraged to **customize them** based on your organizational structure, business needs, and the criticality of the services in question.

BIA Information Gathering

SN	Names of Business Process Application	Associated IT Application	Application Function	Is Application running 24*7	Any Seasonal Variations peak /Critical time	Service Level Agreements	Department Dependencies	OEM dependency
1								
2								

BIA Recovery Time Strategy

SN	Impact	With any existing workarounds in place, what is the impact over time if the application was unavailable					
		4 hrs	1 day	2 days	1 week	1 month	Justification
1	No impact						
	Minor						
	Moderate						
	Major						
	Critical						

Figure 18 BIA Information Gathering and BIA Recovery Templates

BIA Impact Definition

Impact Category	Definition
Revenue loss	Loss of business during the time of disruption
Addon Cost	Temporary staffing, overtime, equipment, services
Regulatory and Legal	Fines, penalties, compliance issues, contractual obligations, financial liabilities
Customer Service	Termination or reduction of service level (internal of external), live operators vs. automated response
Reputation	Public image, shareholder relations, market share
Loss of productivity	Utilization of professional on job due to system down
Loss of Efficiency	Shift operations from automation to manual task

4. Challenges and risks of conducting a BIA

Let's face it-conducting a Business Impact Analysis isn't a walk in the park. With the increasing number of enterprise applications, business processes, and their interdependencies, things can quickly get complex. Add to that the mix of cross-functional teams, external vendors, and third-party tools, and you've got a pretty tangled web to untangle.

Here are some common challenges and risks you might run into:

- **Incomplete or inconsistent information:** Different departments might have varying levels of documentation or knowledge, leading to gaps in the data collected
- **Lack of ownership:** Without clearly defined process owners, it can be tough to gather accurate inputs or validate impact assessments
- **Underestimated interdependencies:** Business functions rarely work in silos. Overlooking how systems or teams rely on one another, can cause blind spots in the analysis
- **Resistance from teams:** BIA exercises require time and focus. Business units often see it as "extra work" and may deprioritize participation
- **Poorly defined impact criteria:** If the impact of downtime isn't measured against clear parameters (financial, operational, reputational), then the analysis becomes subjective and unreliable
- **Dynamic environment:** Applications and processes change frequently-what's true today may not hold tomorrow. BIA needs to keep up

- **Absence of proper tools** , such as qualitative or quantitative ratings, scales, matrices, or models, to measure and compare the impact of different disruptions on different criteria, such as financial loss, customer satisfaction, legal compliance, or operational efficiency
- **Challenge in Reporting** to management in a way that resonates with the decision maker , and while ensuring its clarify and accuracy
- **Limited senior management buy-in:** Without top-down support, the BIA effort can lose momentum or be seen as a checkbox exercise rather than a strategic activity

To overcome these challenges, organizations should treat BIA as a collaborative and iterative effort, supported by senior leadership and embedded within the broader risk management and business continuity planning framework,

5. Template of BCP / DR Policy for reference

A sample template of a generic BCP /DR policy is presented below:

Objective:

Ensure the organization's critical business operations continue during disruptions and are restored to normalcy within acceptable timeframes, minimizing impact on business, stakeholders, and customers.

1.1 Scope

This policy applies to:

- All critical and non-critical business processes, systems, and IT assets.
- Personnel responsible for BCP/DR planning, execution, and testing
- External dependencies, such as third-party service providers and critical vendors

1.2 Policy Statements

1.2.1 Defining Recovery Time Objectives (RTO) and Recovery Point Objectives (RPO)

- **Establish Recovery Time Objectives (RTO):** The maximum acceptable time to restore operations after a disruption
- **Define Recovery Point Objectives (RPO):** The maximum tolerable period for data loss due to an incident
- Classify systems and applications based on criticality and assign RTOs and RPOs accordingly

- Review and update RTOs and RPOs annually or when significant changes occur

1.2.2 Conducting Business Impact Analysis (BIA)

- Perform a Business Impact Analysis (BIA) to:
  - Identify critical business functions and interdependencies
  - Assess the potential financial, reputational, and operational impact of disruptions
  - Prioritize recovery efforts based on criticality and risk
- Update the BIA whenever there are significant changes in business processes or IT infrastructure

1.2.3 Developing and Maintaining BCP/DR Plans

- Document detailed Business Continuity Plans (BCP) and Disaster Recovery Plans (DRP) for all critical processes and systems, including:
  - Emergency contact lists for key personnel and vendors
  - Procedures for communication during disruptions
  - Steps for activating recovery sites or systems
  - Specific recovery procedures for critical applications, data, and infrastructure
- Ensure plans are accessible to authorized personnel and secured against unauthorized access

1.2.4 Regular Testing of BCP/DR Plans

- Test BCP/DR plans at least annually to evaluate their effectiveness, including:
  - Table top exercises for simulating disruption scenarios
  - Full-scale tests of recovery procedures for critical systems and data
- Involve third-party vendors and service providers in testing if they play a critical role in recovery
- Document test results, identify gaps, and implement corrective actions

1.2.5 Ensuring Awareness and Training

- Conduct regular training and awareness sessions for employees to familiarize them with their roles during disruptions
- Train key personnel on the activation and execution of BCP/DR procedures

1.2.6 Continuous Improvement

- Review BCP/DR plans annually or after a disruption or test exercise
- Incorporate lessons learned and emerging risks to enhance plan effectiveness

1.3 Roles and Responsibilities

Business Continuity Manager

- Develop, maintain, and update BCP/DR plans
- Coordinate BIA activities and define RTOs/RPOs with input from stakeholders.
- Organize and oversee testing exercises

IT Disaster Recovery Team

- Implement recovery procedures for IT systems and infrastructure during disruptions
- Ensure backups are available and restorable within defined RPOs

CISO

- Ensure alignment of BCP/DR plans with cybersecurity objectives
- Oversee the testing of cyber-resilience aspects, such as ransomware recovery

Employees

- Understand their roles and responsibilities as defined in the BCP/DR plans
- Participate in training and testing exercises as required

Internal Audit Team

- Audit the BCP/DR plans and processes for compliance and effectiveness.
- Review test results and provide feedback for improvement

6. Conclusion: Risk Assessment versus Business Impact Assessment

Risk Assessment (RA) and Business Impact Analysis (BIA) may sound similar-and yes, they do share some common ground, but they serve different purposes within a Governance, Risk, and Compliance (GRC) framework.

Risk Assessment is all about identifying threats and vulnerabilities that could affect your IT and business environment-whether internal, external, technological, or compliance-driven. It helps you answer the question: *What could go wrong, and how likely is it?*

Business Impact Analysis, on the other hand, digs into how bad things can get if your critical processes or systems are disrupted. It's less about the cause and more about the *consequences*. It helps determine: *If this goes down, then how much will it hurt the business?*

While they differ in approach:

- RA is risk-centric, evaluating likelihood and severity of potential threats.
- BIA is impact-centric, estimating business fallout from disruptions.

In practice, especially for SMEs, it might seem tempting to skip one over the other, but that's risky in itself. Both RA and BIA should run in parallel, complementing each other to build a full picture of organizational resilience.

Together, they help prioritize investments, tighten controls, and strengthen recovery planning-ultimately helping the organization withstand and bounce back from disruptions

Areas Covered	**BIA (Business Impact Assessment)**	**RA (Risk Assessment)**
Major Attention	How disruptions can impact	What are the likelihood of occurrence of the threats
Scope Boundaries	Which critical applications are to be considered to be part of exercise	Address all potential threats and vulnerabilities which can be considered
Deliverables	How effectively within how much time one can recover	Rating and ranking of risk and issue and how it can be possibly mitigated
Approach and Methodology	Rely on data collection, and use both quantitative and qualitative approach to analyse the operations impact, from business perspective	RA includes risk identification, analysis, evaluation and treatment

Figure 19 BIA and RA comparison

As we continue to build a comprehensive GRC framework, there's another critical layer that demands focused attention-**Data Privacy and Protection**. In an era where data is currency and regulations like GDPR, PDPL, and DPDPA are reshaping how organizations manage personal information, assessing privacy risks becomes just as vital as cyber risks or operational impacts.

In the upcoming section, we'll explore how **Privacy Impact Assessments (PIA)** and **Data Protection Impact Assessments (DPIA)** fit into the broader GRC picture.

Chapter

6

GRC and Data Security Governance

1. Introduction

In today's interconnected world, **data is everywhere**-being created, accessed, shared, and stored across borders and systems. While traditional Information Security Governance has always focused on the **CIA triad-Confidentiality, Integrity, and Availability,** a fourth pillar now demands equal attention: **Privacy**.

This is where Data Security Governance (DSG) comes into play. DSG focuses on managing data security across its entire lifecycle-from the moment it's created or collected, through its usage and transfer, to its eventual archival or disposal.

Just as we need to assess the **risks to IT assets** and conduct **business process impact assessments,** we also need to review and conduct **Data Protection and Privacy Impact Assessments (DPIA)** to understand how personal and sensitive data is being handled, and to ensure compliance with evolving global privacy regulations.

In this section, we will explore the key dimensions of **Data Security Governance within a GRC framework,** focusing on how organizations should govern the handling, usage, transfer, and storage of digital data-securely and responsibly.

2. GRC ad Data Security Governance

As organizations increasingly rely on digital ecosystems to drive business, **data has become the new oil**-a critical asset that fuels innovation and operations. But with great data comes great responsibility. That responsibility includes:

- Ensuring the security of data from unauthorized access or breaches
- Guaranteeing the privacy of individuals whose personal data is processed, and
- Meeting compliance obligations under regulations like GDPR, PDPL, DPDPA, CCPA, and others

Before diving deeper, let's clarify commonly interchanged but distinct concepts:

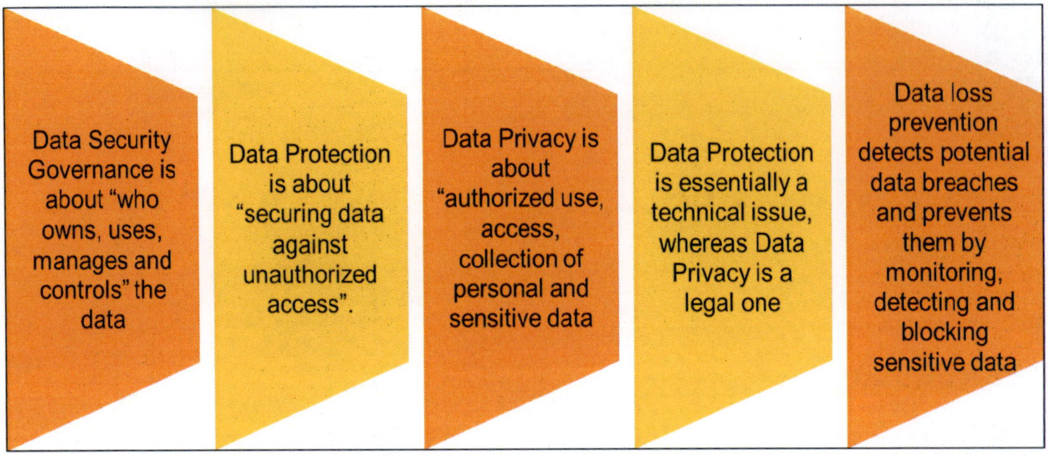

Figure 20 GRC in Data Security Governance

Why Data Security Governance Matters in GRC

The Data Security Governance Risk and Compliance framework is a structured approach to ensure that data is:

- Handled transparently and securely
- Processed in line with business objectives and regulatory requirements
- Protected throughout its journey-from creation to deletion

Although DSG can be considered as a subset of Information Security Governance, it deserves a parallel track due to its complexity, legal obligations, and criticality to stakeholder trust.

Building a DSG Framework: Top-Down Approach

When implementing a DSG framework, a top-down strategy is essential. Here's why:

- DSG is aligned to business requirement, organizational policies and in lines with Information Security Governance program
- DSG program should follow through the chain of data flow within the organization right from data generation to transfer to flow and subsequent recycle or disposal
- Data Analysis and reusage plays a major role in today's Next Gen AI environment in which both structured, unstructured data is required

- DSG also extends in looking at the data security areas, while Data is in motion, Data is in transit and Data at rest mode
- DSG comprises of looking at Data Privacy & Protection, and Data Classification & Categorization which are the 2 main areas
- DSG also needs to address concerns around Data Localization as per regional requirements
- DSG can viewed as program running horizontally across the enterprise with a wrap of ISG running vertically

The above points have been summarized in the schematic diagram as below:

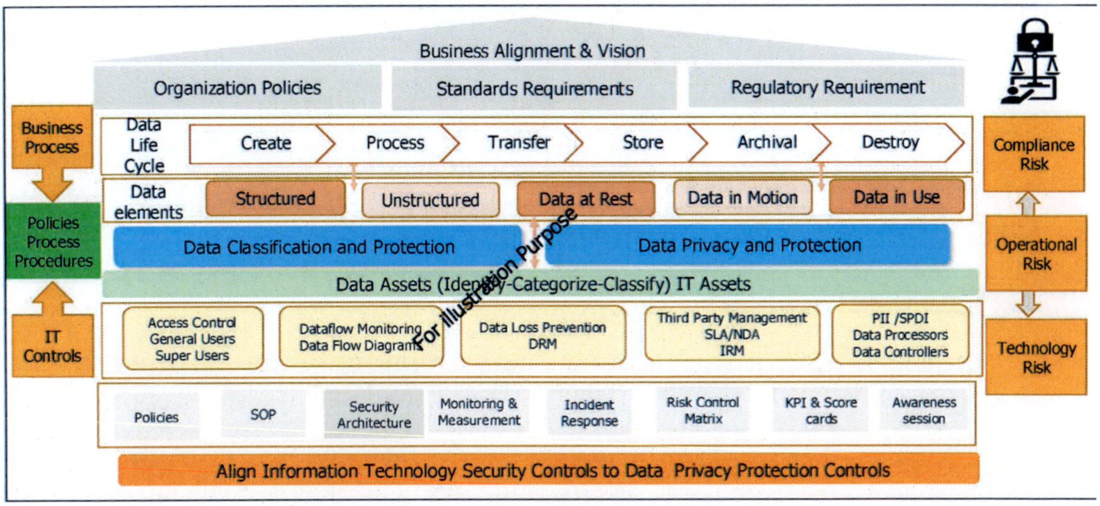

Figure 21 DSG and ISG Representation

In the subsequent sections of the DSG we will look at the 4 strategy areas covering:

- **Data Classification and Categorization** (around data assetization)
- **Data Privacy and Protection** (around protecting personal information)
- **Data Operations Management** (around data security controls)
- **Data Governance and Management** (around policies and procedures)

Figures below show a representation of how DSG quadrants can be viewed:

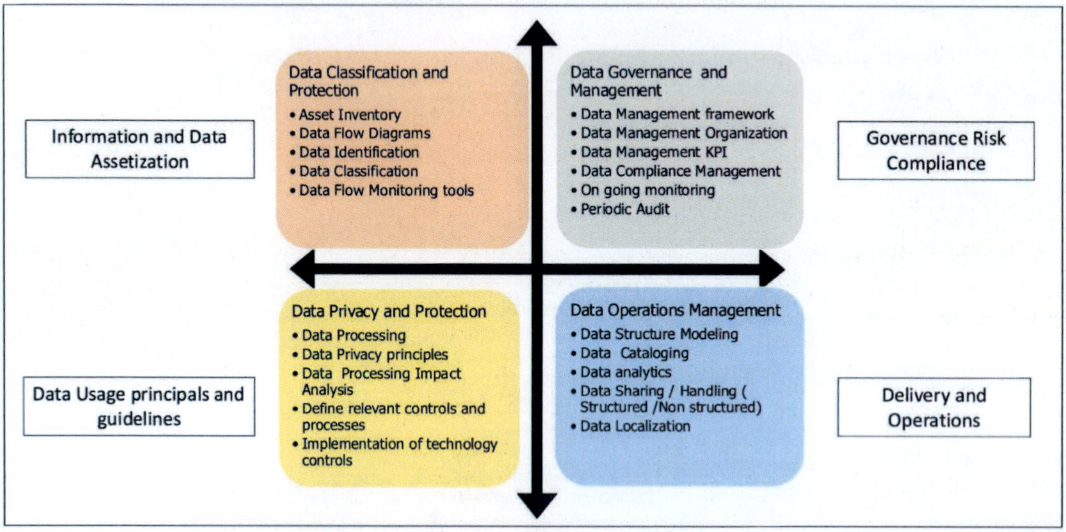

Figure 22 DSG 4-Quadrant Approach

3. Data Classification and Protection

What is Data Classification?

In the modern digital enterprise, **data is constantly on the move**-flowing between users, systems, departments, and even across borders. But not all data is created equal.

Some data might be public and harmless, if exposed. Other data-like customer personal details, financial records, or trade secrets-could result in major financial loss, legal consequences, or reputational damage if mishandled.

That's where Data Classification comes in.

Data classification is the **systematic process of identifying, tagging, and organizing data** based on its sensitivity, criticality, and importance to the business. It serves as the first step in protecting information-before implementing access controls or encryption.

Why Data Classification Matters?

Without classification, organizations are flying blind. You can't protect what you haven't identified. Proper classification helps to:

- **Enforce access control** based on the "need to know" principle.
- **Reduce the risk** of data leaks, breaches, or misuse

- **Support compliance** with regulations such as GDPR, DPDP Act, HIPAA, etc.
- **Guide protection measures** like encryption, masking, or data loss prevention (DLP)
- Streamline incident response when a data breach occurs

In short, **classification informs action**-what needs to be locked down, who can access it, and how it should be handled at every stage of its lifecycle.

Types of Data Classification

Data can be classified in multiple ways depending on the organization's industry, regulatory environment, and risk appetite. A common three - tiered classification scheme looks like this:

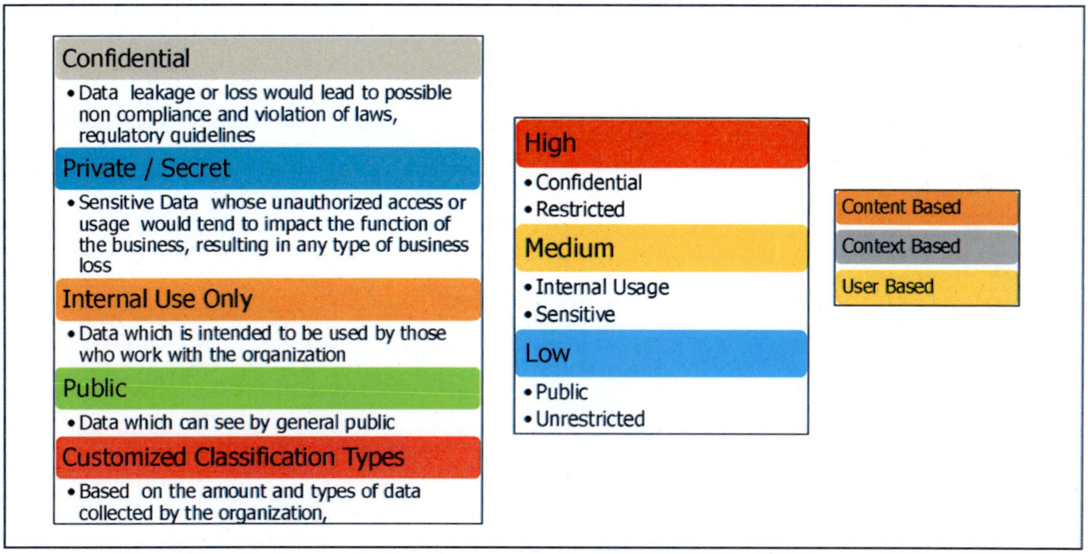

Figure 23 DSG Data Classification Types for illustration only

Why Data Classification?

- Adherence to CIA principles – enables to follow the practice of deploying security controls on need to know need to do basis and based on the type of data, access can be granted, usage can be defined and same can be monitored and tracked
- Data Workflow – enables to identify flow of data, thus addressing the needs of ensuring security while data is in rest, motion and transit

- Compliance – structured methodology will help organization to address the different requirements of regulatory compliance based on organizations vertical
- Organizing data for optimal usage - enabling to relook at organization's storage requirements and avoid duplication of data across multiple locations leading to efficient data management
- Risk Assessment – on going monitoring and measurement further aide organization in its process of identifying possible risks and proactively take steps to mitigate
- Build awareness within user – this fosters a culture of security with the organization and also helps end users to ensure necessary do's and dont's are addressed effectively while using different types of classified data

How to do Data Classification?

- Enterprise wise data classification program can be done manually using a traditional checklist-based approach, or alternately, automated tools can be also used to handle complex distributed IT environments
- For small medium enterprise segment, it is better to adopt a manual method and for large enterprise recommend to adopt a hybrid method
- Manual approach enables to have a better touch point at possible areas which may have missed by the limitation of automated tools; hence a hybrid approach is more preferable
- While doing data classification, other area that needs to be addressed is to understand the requirements of all compliance, especially if dealing with Data Privacy, Data Localization. Many organizations will require compliance to multiple such as GDPR, HIPAA, SAMA. As Laws keep changing or amended, hence one has to see that latest releases are taken in to consideration
- One can take either business process-based approach or department approach as per size of the organization. Departmental approach may possibly provide a granular level detail. A business process may function across multiple teams, hence we will be able to get different viewpoints of data types and classification. One of the challenges in adopting a business process approach is extracting relevant details from unstructured data, which must be considered during the exercise.
- End to end documentation of different policies, procedures, handling guidelines should be developed along with an incident response plan

Workflow to a data classification exercise is as follows:

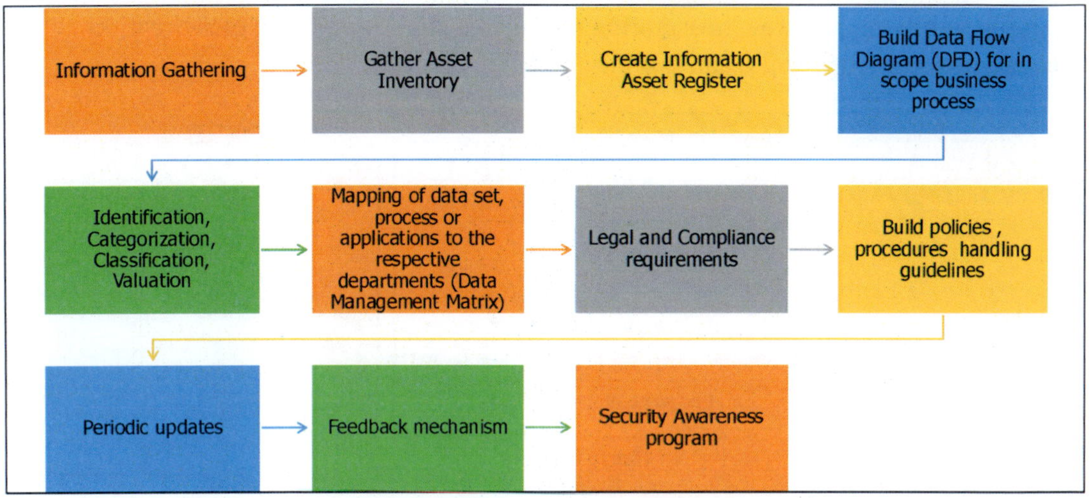

Figure 24 Data Classification Workflow

4. Data Classification Sample template

A sample template used for information gathering and doing data classfication across different business functions, can comprise of :

Data Channels Sources		
Communication Channels & Response	End Point Channel	USB - storage
		Exempted users for USB (Domain ID)
		CD- ROM
		Exempted users for CD-Rom (Domain ID)
		Endpoint Printing
		Exempted users for Printing (Domain ID)
		Endpoint Web (HTTP/s)
		Exempted Internal Site for Endpoint web (Email ID)
		Screenshots
		Exempted users for Screen Shot (Username)
	Network Channel	Network Web (HTTP/S)
		Network Email
		Exempted users for Network Email (Username)
		Instant Messaging (Internet)
		Instant Messaging User ID
		FTP
		Exempted FTP Server Hostname or IP
Information Asset Handling of Eletronic Data		Storage
		Transfer
		Disposal

Input Source	
Data / Document Type	EXCEL
	IMAGE
	CSV
	DOC
	PDF
	TXT
	PPT
	RAR
	Other Format
Information Classification Analysis	
Impact Parameters	Legal Impact
	Reputation Impact
	Financial Impact
	Operational Impact
Information Handling	
Data in state	Storage
	Transfer
	Disposal

Figure 25 Data Classification Information Gathering

5. Data Privacy and Protection

In today's digital world, **enterprise IT systems are the vaults** that store and manage both critical business information and personal data. From banking apps to healthcare platforms and e-commerce websites, personal data is being collected, processed, and transmitted more than ever before-especially with the surge in **AI-powered solutions** and cloud-based technologies.

But with this convenience comes risk.

There's always been the danger that such information could be **misused, accessed without consent,** or even fall into the wrong hands. These concerns have led to the creation of data privacy regulations globally-laws designed to safeguard how personal data is collected, stored, processed, and shared by both public and private entities.

What is Data Privacy?

Data Privacy is the practice of ensuring that personal, sensitive, or Personnel identifiable information is :

- Collected with proper consent
- Used only for legitimate, authorized purposes
- Kept secure from unauthorized access
- Processed transparently with accountability

Personal data refers to any information that can directly or indirectly identify an individual. This includes:

- **PII (Personally Identifiable Information):**
  - Full name, email address, phone number, PAN, passport number, driver's license, etc.
- **SPDI (Sensitive Personal Data or Information):**
  - Aadhaar number, credit/debit card details, financial information, biometric data, medical history, mental health information, etc

Such data, if exposed or mishandled, could be **misused for fraud, identity theft, or even profiling,** making it imperative to implement strong data privacy safeguards.

At the heart of every effective privacy program are **three foundational principles: Consent-Transparency-Security.** The details of the principles are explained in subsequent sections below

Why Data Privacy Laws Exist?

With personal data moving rapidly across borders, and AI/ML models learning from user behavior, there is a large global momentum to establish strong privacy frameworks. Governments and regulators are also pushing organizations to **build trust,** ensure **transparency,** and uphold the **privacy rights of individuals.**

These laws not only aim to protect users from cyber threats and misuse but also give them more control over their personal information-such as the right to know how it's used, to whom it's shared, and to request its deletion.

Key Global Data Privacy Laws

Here's a quick snapshot of major region-specific privacy regulations:

General Data Protection Regulation Act (GDPR) , for EU countries	California Privacy Regulation Act (CPRA) for US region
China's Personal Information Protection Law (PIPL)	Digital Personal Data Protection Act India
Brazil's General Law for the Protection of Privacy	Protection of Personal Information Act (POPI Act) South Africa
Personal Data Protection Law (PDPL) Saudi Arabia	Privacy Act , Australia

The above are examples of privacy laws of few countries, similarly other regions of the world have some adaption of the above laws is some form or the other. Some the terms which can commonly referred Data Privacy are:

- **Data Subjects:** Owners, Individuals whose personal data is being collected or processed
- **Data Controllers/ Fiduciaries:** Organizations that determine how and why personal data is processed
- **Data Processors/ Fiduciaries :** Third-party entities that handle data on behalf of the controller

To safeguard **Personally Identifiable Information (PII)** and **Sensitive Personal Data or Information (SPDI)** from unauthorized access, misuse, or disclosure, organizations must adopt a **defined set of privacy principles and controls.**

While the **specific number and nature of these controls** may vary depending on the country-specific privacy regulations (such as GDPR, DPDPA, CCPA, etc.), several **fundamental principles remain consistent** across most frameworks.

Organizations must proactively:

- **Assess** their data processing activities
- **Build** robust data protection practices
- **Implement** necessary controls
- And **Maintain** a Data Security Governance (DSG) framework continuously

The figure below illustrates **key common privacy principles** that are foundational across major data protection laws and should be considered while designing or enhancing an organization's DSG framework.

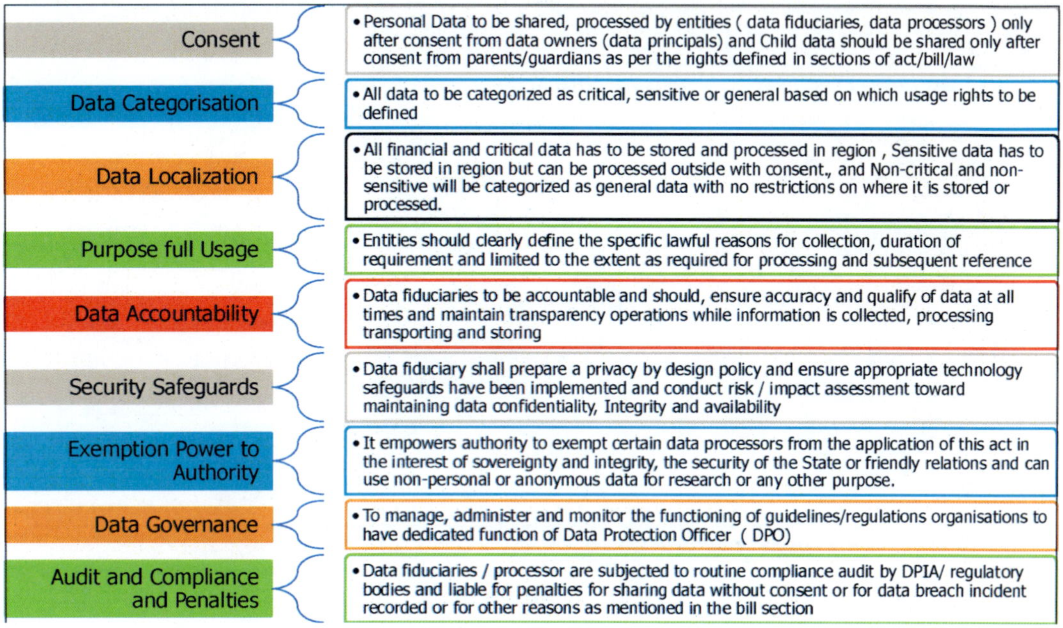

Figure 26 Data Privacy Governing Principles

6. Data Privacy Impact Assessment

In today's data-driven business environment, organizations are custodians of a vast amount of **personal and sensitive data.** With the growing risk of **data misuse, identity theft, and corporate information breaches,** it is no longer optional-but essential-to assess how personal data is handled.

As mandated by many **regional privacy regulations** (such as GDPR, DPDPA, CCPA, etc.), organizations are required to carry out a **Data Privacy Impact Assessment (DPIA).** This is a **risk-based evaluation** designed to:

- Identify potential **privacy risks** in data processing activities,
- Ensure **compliance** with privacy principles,
- And embed **privacy-by-design** into business processes and systems.

DPIA is especially critical when organizations introduce new technologies, modify existing systems, or process data that may significantly impact individual privacy rights.

The purpose of a DPIA is to ensure that **privacy risks are addressed early,** controls are appropriately implemented, and the organization remains **aligned with legal obligations** across its operations.

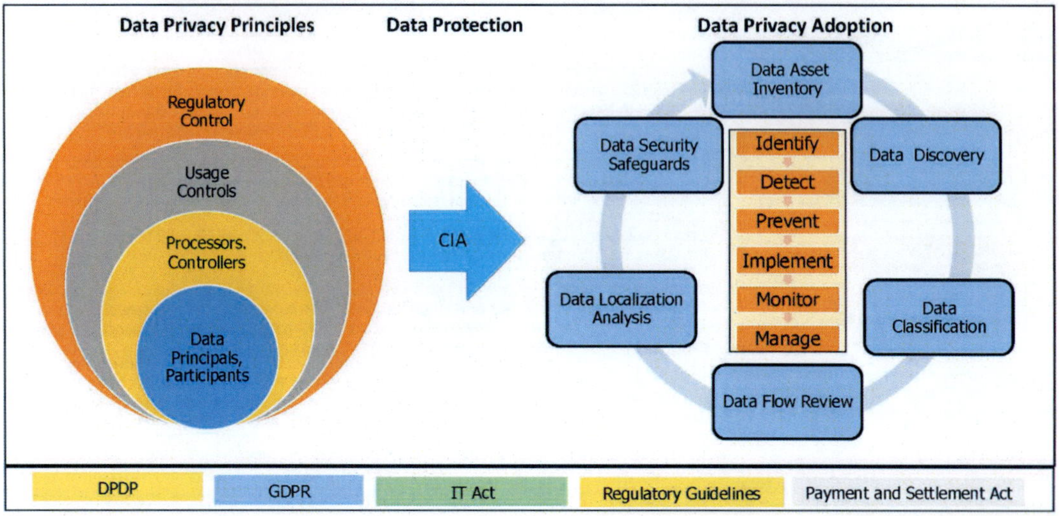

Figure 27 Data Privacy and Protection

A template of typical Data Privacy Impact Assessment used for data collection is presented below

Data Collection and Processing					Data Rention and Accurancy			Data Fiduciaries			
Data set name	Data subjects	Grounds for Processing	Purpose of Processing	Used for Marketing?	Retention period (months)	Access restrictions	Accuracy (%)	Controller or Processor?	Joint Controller?	Other controllers (if Joint Controller)	Automated Processing ?
						ty					

Data Categories				Data Processing Location				Security Complaince	
Personal Data	Special Category Data	Genetic/ Biometric/ Health Data	Children's Data	Obtained Directly or Indirectly?	Data Location	Outsourced Processing?	Cross-Border Processing?	Privacy Laws	Auditing and monitoring

Figure 28 Data Privacy Impact Assessment Template for illustration only

DPIA in Alignment with BPIA and Data Classification

A smart approach for organizations looking to optimize effort and maximize output is to **align the Data Privacy Impact Assessment (DPIA)** with **Business Process Impact Assessment (BPIA)** and **Data Classification exercises.** Why?

- **The audience is the same:** business process owners, data custodians, and system owners
- **The outputs complement each other:** BPIA identifies critical processes, Data Classification tags sensitive data, and DPIA uncovers privacy risks in data handling
- Conducting them together improves efficiency, avoids duplication, and provides a **comprehensive view** of operational risk, data sensitivity, and compliance requirements

This combined strategy not only strengthens your organization's data protection posture, but also lays the groundwork for a sound Data Governance framework.

7. Data Governance and Management Policy

A sample Data Privacy and Protection policy is placed below for reference only. This may be required to be customised to adopt to the individual needs and requirement.

Objective: Ensure compliance with applicable data protection laws and safeguard sensitive information, minimizing risks of unauthorized access, disclosure, and data breaches.

1.1 Scope This policy applies to:

- All personally identifiable information (PII) and sensitive data managed by the organization
- Data collection, storage, transmission, processing, and disposal activities
- Both physical and electronic data, including backups and offsite storage
- Compliance with relevant data protection regulations (e.g., GDPR, PDPL, CCPA)

1.2 Policy Statements

1.2.1 Enforce Data Classification and Handling Policies

- **Objective:** Ensure that data is classified based on its sensitivity and is handled in accordance with its classification
- **Key Controls:**
  - o **Data Classification:** Implement a classification scheme categorizing data based on sensitivity (e.g., public, internal, confidential, restricted). All data must be classified at creation or intake.

- o **Data Handling Procedures:** Define specific data handling procedures for each data classification. Sensitive and confidential data must be subject to stricter controls, such as limited access, encryption, and logging.
- o **Access Control:** Access to sensitive data should be granted on a need-to-know basis, according to the principle of least privilege. Regularly review and adjust access levels to ensure compliance.
- o **Data Retention and Disposal:** Establish clear data retention policies specifying the duration data is retained and secure methods for data disposal, including deletion or anonymization for data that is no longer required.

1.2.2 Encrypt Sensitive Data at Rest and in Transit

- **Objective:** Protect sensitive data from unauthorized access by ensuring it is encrypted during storage and transmission.
- **Key Controls:**
  - o **Encryption at Rest:** All sensitive data stored in databases, file systems, and backups must be encrypted using strong encryption standards (e.g., AES-256) to prevent unauthorized access in case of data breaches or physical theft of devices.
  - o **Encryption in Transit:** All sensitive data transmitted over networks, including email, web applications, and internal communications, must be encrypted using secure protocols such as TLS (Transport Layer Security) or VPNs (Virtual Private Networks) to safeguard data during transmission.
  - o **Encryption Key Management:** Implement robust key management practices, ensuring encryption keys are stored securely, rotated regularly, and only accessible by authorized personnel or systems.

1.2.3 Provide Mechanisms for Data Subject Rights Management

- **Objective:** Enable individuals to exercise their data protection rights and ensure the organization complies with relevant data protection laws
- **Key Controls:**
  - o **Data Subject Requests:** Establish processes to handle requests from data subjects, including requests for access, rectification, deletion, or

portability of their personal data. Ensure these requests are addressed within the legally defined timelines.

- o **Consent Management:** Obtain explicit consent from data subjects for the collection, processing, or sharing of their personal data where required by law. Implement processes for tracking and managing consent, including withdrawal of consent.
- o **Privacy Policy and Notices:** Provide transparent privacy policies and notices to individuals regarding the collection and use of their data. Ensure these policies are easily accessible and regularly updated.
- o **Data Minimization:** Collect only the necessary amount of personal data for specific purposes and avoid storing excessive or irrelevant data.
- o **Data Anonymization/Pseudonymization:** Where possible, implement anonymization or pseudonymization techniques to reduce the risks associated with data exposure.

1.2.4 Implement Data Loss Prevention (DLP) Measures

- **Objective:** Prevent the unauthorized access, leakage, or transfer of sensitive data
- **Key Controls:**
  - o **Data Loss Prevention Tools:** Implement DLP tools to monitor and restrict the movement of sensitive data within the organization's network and to external environments (e.g., USB devices, email, cloud storage).
  - o **Policy Enforcement:** Define and enforce DLP policies to prevent unauthorized sharing or transfer of sensitive data, such as restrictions on copying, printing, or emailing confidential information.
  - o **Monitoring and Alerts:** Continuously monitor data flows and implement automated alerts to detect and respond to unauthorized attempts to access, modify, or transfer sensitive data.

1.2.5 Regular Data Protection Impact Assessments (DPIAs)

- **Objective:** Assess the privacy risks associated with data processing activities and take steps to mitigate them

- **Key Controls:**
  - o **DPIA Requirement:** Conduct DPIA for high-risk data processing activities, especially those that involve new technologies, large-scale processing of sensitive data, or when data processing could result in significant privacy risks to data subjects.
  - o **Risk Mitigation:** Identify and assess potential privacy risks, then implement mitigation strategies (e.g., enhancing security measures, anonymizing data) to reduce the risks to an acceptable level.
  - o **Third-Party Processing**: Include third-party processors in DPIAs to ensure they meet the same privacy and security standards as the organization itself.

1.2.6 Data Privacy Training and Awareness

- **Objective:** Ensure that employees are aware of their data protection responsibilities and equipped with the knowledge to protect sensitive data
- **Key Controls:**
  - o **Training Programs:** Provide regular data protection and privacy training for all employees, covering topics such as the organization's data protection policies, the importance of confidentiality, and how to handle sensitive data securely.
  - o **Employee Accountability:** Hold employees accountable for adhering to data protection practices, with consequences for breaches or violations of privacy policies.
  - o **Role-Specific Training:** Offer specialized training for staff involved in data processing, IT, legal compliance, and other relevant areas to ensure they are fully aware of their responsibilities and best practices in handling sensitive data.

1.3 Roles and Responsibilities

- **Data Protection Officer (DPO):** Oversee data protection activities, ensure compliance with data protection laws, and act as the point of contact for data subjects regarding their rights
- **Compliance and Legal Team:** Ensure that the organization's data protection policies and practices align with relevant regulations (e.g., GDPR, PDPL, CCPA) and provide legal advice on privacy-related matters.

- **IT and Security Teams:** Implement technical controls, such as encryption and DLP, to protect sensitive data and ensure its security during storage and transmission.
- **HR and Employee Training Teams:** Ensure employees are trained in data protection and privacy practices and hold them accountable for data protection responsibilities.
- **Data Owners and Custodians:** Ensure that sensitive data is classified, handled, and protected according to its sensitivity and the organization's data protection policies.

By adhering to these practices, the organization ensures the protection of sensitive data and the privacy of individuals while complying with applicable data protection laws and regulations. This is template for illustration and may need further customisation as per organisation requirements. Further individual standard operating procedures may be required to be build to address work specific requirements .

Final Thought

Data is power-but with power comes responsibility.

Organizations that handle personal data must respect the privacy of individuals, and implement practices aligned not just with compliance, but with ethical data stewardship.

8. Data Protection Technologies platform

Technology plays a **critical enabler role** in ensuring that data privacy and protection principles are enforced consistently across the organization. To bridge the gap between policy and practice, organizations must deploy a **range of data protection technologies** tailored to their business environment and compliance needs.

These tools help safeguard personal and sensitive data, control access, prevent leakage, and ensure that data is handled in line with applicable privacy laws.

The figure below presents an **indicative list of technologies** and their core usage areas to support a comprehensive **Data Security Governance (DSG)** program

Data Access Governance	• Determine who owns , uses and has access to sensitive information
Data Discovery	• Locate sensitive information on IT resources
Information Rights Management	• Restrict or provided limited access to documents
Disk Encryption	• Encrypt data on drives, external hard disk drives
Device Control	• Monitor, encrypt and prevent transfers of sensitive information to removable disk drive
Data Loss Prevention	• Monitor, Scans end points to identify , detect and prevent sensitive information from being transferred
Data and Classification	• Allows users to classify the type of data which is being used or generated , edited or sent via email
Gateway Encryption	• Provide a method to encrypt emails data while in transit
Mobile Device Management	• Enforce policy , segregate sensitive information and provide remote wipe capabilities for mobile devices
Document Archiving	• Provide a security and efficient process for storing and retrieving archived sensitive information
Tokenization and Masking	• Secure confidential information while preserving business processes and minimizing application recoding

Figure 29 Data Security Technologies Snap Shot

9. Conclusion

Data Security Governance (DSG) stands as a vital pillar within the broader **Governance, Risk, and Compliance (GRC)** framework. In today's digital-first world, **data is the new oil** - powering innovation, customer engagement, and business growth. But with this value comes significant responsibility.

As data flows across systems, networks, and borders - often carrying sensitive or personal information - ensuring its **protection from unauthorized access, misuse, or theft** becomes a critical obligation. Whether stored at rest or transferred electronically, data must be safeguarded through both **well-defined policies and robust technical controls.**

By embedding a strong DSG framework that aligns with **regulatory requirements and privacy laws,** organizations can:

- Build **digital trust** with customers and regulators
- Reduce the risk of data breaches and legal penalties
- And ensure that data handling is **secure, transparent, and compliant** across its lifecycle

Ultimately, DSG is not just a compliance mandate - it's a strategic business enabler.

Chapter

7

GRC and Access Management

1. Introduction

In modern enterprises, users access IT resources through diverse platforms, devices, and methods. These users can include internal employees, third-party vendors, contractors, and even applications that interact automatically. To ensure secure access while maintaining operational efficiency, organizations assign different levels of access based on the **user's role and the specific tasks** to be performed on systems such as servers, network devices, applications, and databases.

Effective Access Management is crucial for:

- Protecting sensitive information from unauthorized use or disclosure
- Enforcing internal controls
- Preventing security breaches
- And complying with regulatory and audit requirements

2. What is Access Management

Access Management refers to the framework of policies, processes, and tools that govern how users (or identities) gain authorized access to IT resources. It includes three key components:

a. Identity and Access Management (IAM)

IAM is a comprehensive framework combining **identity verification, role-based access, and authentication mechanisms.** It ensures the **right individuals** access the **right resources** at the **right time** and for the **right reasons.** IAM supports:

- Role-Based Access Control (RBAC)
- Multi-Factor Authentication (MFA)

- Lifecycle management of user identities
- Grouping based on business / application needs

IAM tools define user roles based on job functions, business units, or application needs, streamlining both access provisioning and governance.

b. User Access Management (UAM)

UAM is a subset of IAM, focusing specifically on managing individual user accounts, roles, and permissions. It handles basic access provisioning such as:

- Username and password-based login
- Two-Factor Authentication (2FA)
- Granting or revoking access based on user responsibilities

UAM primarily covers standard users accessing enterprise systems without administrative privileges.

c. Privileged Access Management (PAM)

PAM is concerned with users who have **elevated or administrative privileges,** such as:

- System administrators
- Database administrators
- Network engineers

These users typically manage critical infrastructure and thus require **restricted, monitored, and audited** access. PAM tools support:

- Just-In-Time (JIT) access
- Session monitoring
- Password vaulting and rotation
- Audit logs of privileged activity

Together, these three components help organizations establish **granular, controlled, and auditable access** to their information systems.

3. User Access Methods

Organizations adopt a range of user access methods depending on:

- The size of the organization

- Number and complexity of business applications
- User types (internal, external, third-party)
- Security and compliance requirements

Some of the different types of access control methods deployed by organisations include:

- **Standard Desktop based logon** – for very small organisation who are not having any servers or business applications and using only cloud-based SaaS platforms
- **Domain based Username**-Password login through organisation level active directory structure
- **Email id-based login** which is integrated with activity directory
- **Data base driven username password logon** for applications hosted in client server mode or through web portal
- Multiple username password combination for multiple applications
- System specific login process for network devices, security devices
- Single-Signon (SSO) tool to integrate all types of user logon into one, SSO works generally along with IAM , PAM
- Muti factor authentication such as One time password (OTP) , RFID cards, biometric are some of the options which are be considered as per complexity
- Certificate-based authentication using digital certificates issued by a trusted authority i,e a method, which exchanges shared and secret digital key such as PKI to address non repudiation
- Cloud platforms SaaS based access as per the platform specific requirement

Before diving deeper into access control models and technologies, it's essential to understand a few core access management terms:

- Each type of devices ,servers , applications which requires login credential can be terms as an ACCOUNT in assess management
- Each type of users i.e. internal , external , customers, oem who logs into the accounts can be termed as USER of the IT resources and need user-based access controls
- A group of similar users who have same functions and perform same type of tasks or operations can be grouped under a common ROLE and thus need role base access control. E.g. System administrator, network administrator role, business users etc

- **Authentication:** Verifying a user's identity (e.g., password, OTP, biometric)
- **Authorization:** Granting permission to access specific resources
- **Access Control List (ACL):** A list that defines what each user/group is allowed to access
- **Session Management:** Controlling and monitoring user sessions
- **Least Privilege:** Granting the minimal access needed to perform a function
- **Segregation of Duties (SoD):** Ensuring no single user has conflicting responsibilities that could lead to fraud
- In many cases granular level of access can be further defined such as read, write, modify which leads to a further category of ACCESS level-based control

The schematic below presents a workflow showing relationship between different

- Identities in the system ,
- Type of access management platforms,
- And its integration to applications and different platforms for monitoring and management

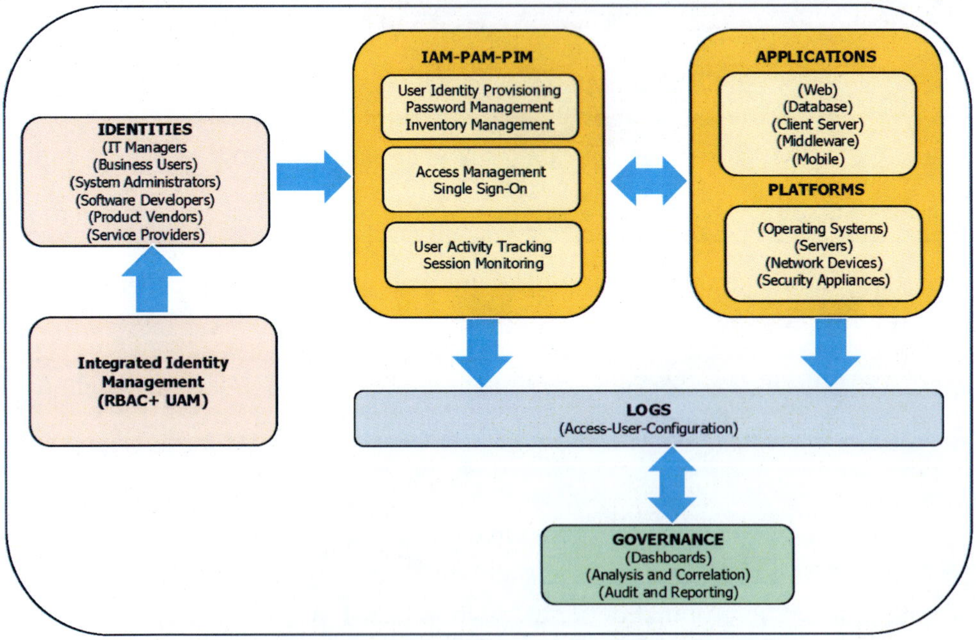

Figure 30 Access Management Identities

In the following sections, we'll explore these in more detail, along with implementation strategies, audit mechanisms, and GRC alignment.

4. Benefits of Access Management Implementation

Access Control Management system when deployed provide fine tunned granular level control at all layers of network covering systems, network, applications and others . To summarise the benefits

- **Visibility of Operational** – monitoring of the usage, tracking user activities helps provide information of how system resources are utilised and address risks due to insiders and outsider timely
- **Deploy Security on need to know need to do basis** – build and deploy and implement granular level controls enabling operational efficiency and enhanced security
- **Third Party Risk Management** – effective deployment of separates Role helps proper identification of 3rd parties who have been provided access
- **Security Culture** – enables build a security awareness indirectly with the users of the system

5. Access Management Policy Template

A sample template of a typical access management policy is provided below for reference only .Based on the individual requirements and needs the same will need to be customised or modified.

Objective: Ensure that only authorized users have appropriate access to systems, applications, and data while preventing unauthorized access, ensuring data integrity, confidentiality, and compliance with regulatory requirements.

1.1 Scope

This policy applies to all:

- **Users**: Employees, contractors, third-party vendors, and privileged users
- **Systems and Applications**: IT infrastructure, databases, and critical/non-critical applications
- **Data Assets:** Sensitive and business-critical information stored or processed within the organization

1.2 Policy Statements

1.2.1 Role-Based Access Control (RBAC)

- Define and implement role-based access control (RBAC) to:
  - o Grant access rights based on job roles and responsibilities.
  - o Enforce the principle of least privilege by limiting access to only what is necessary for a role
  - o Maintain an access control matrix to document roles, privileges, and access levels for all users
- Segregate administrative privileges from regular user accounts to minimize misuse.

1.2.2 Multi-Factor Authentication (MFA)

- Enforce multi-factor authentication (MFA) for accessing:
  - o Critical systems and applications (e.g., financial systems, databases, and privileged accounts)
  - o Remote access points, such as VPNs or cloud services
- Require MFA solutions to include at least two authentication factors (e.g., password + biometric or password + OTP)

1.2.3 Access Request and Approval Process

- Establish a formal access request workflow, including:
  - o Submission of requests via approved channels.
  - o Justification for access
  - o Approval by the respective department head or system owner
- Maintain documentation of all access requests and approvals for auditing purposes

1.2.4 Periodic Access Reviews

- Conduct quarterly reviews of access rights to ensure:
  - o Consistency with job roles and responsibilities
  - o Removal of access for inactive or terminated users

- Involve asset/system owners in access reviews to validate necessity and appropriateness
- Document and address any discrepancies identified during reviews

1.2.5 Revocation of Unnecessary Access

- Revoke access immediately for:
    - Employees leaving the organization.
    - Role changes that no longer require certain privileges
    - Inactive accounts exceeding defined inactivity thresholds
- Implement automated systems for de-provisioning to reduce delays and errors

1.2.6 Logging and Monitoring of Access Activities

- Maintain detailed logs of all access activities, capturing:
    - User IDs, time stamps, system/resource accessed, and activity type
    - Login attempts (successful and failed) and privileged access usage
- Use security information and event management (SIEM) tools to monitor access logs for suspicious activities
- Retain access logs as per regulatory requirements and internal policies (e.g., minimum six months)

1.3 Roles and Responsibilities

System Owners

- Approve access requests and participate in periodic access reviews
- Validate access rights against user roles and responsibilities

IT Team

- Implement access controls, MFA, and automated tools for access management.
- Monitor access logs and escalate anomalies to the CISO

CISO

- Oversee the access control framework and ensure compliance with regulatory requirements

- Periodically review access policies and ensure their alignment with best practices

Employees and Users

- Use assigned credentials responsibly and avoid sharing passwords or tokens
- Report any unauthorized access attempts or security concerns immediately

Internal Audit Team

- Conduct periodic audits of access controls, ensuring adherence to the policy and identifying gaps
- Verify that access logs and reviews are maintained as required

The template is an indicative approach towards building a Assess Management policy and will need further customisation . The granularity will further depend on the overall enterprise size and complexity of functional of the Access Management framework

6. Access Management Standard Operation procedure template

To initiate and streamline the implementation of an **Access Management Framework,** organizations can use a **structured SOP template** as a checklist. This helps in identifying key requirements, designing implementation strategies, and ensuring ongoing monitoring and compliance.

This template provides a high-level view, and can be further customized based on:

- Regional regulatory requirements
- Organizational roles and business processes
- IT infrastructure complexity
- Risk profile and criticality of systems

User Details								
SR.No	User ID	Employee Name	Department	Designation	User Employement Status	Access to what type of systems / App	Access Type	Approval Status
Access Review and Monitoring								
SR.No	Access Granted	Access Review Date	Access Expiry Date	Last Login Date	Dormant Account Status			
Privileged & Sensitive Access Control								
SR.No	Privileged Access Review	What kind of Access are given	Remote Access	Segregation of Duties check	Exception Handling	Access Revoked	Audit findings	Management Review

Figure 31 Access Management Information Gathering template

7. Conclusion

In today's dynamic digital landscape, users-whether internal employees, third-party vendors, or privileged administrators-are continuously interacting with organizational IT resources. Ensuring the **Confidentiality, Integrity, and Availability (CIA)** of these resources is critical to sustaining a secure and compliant operational environment.

To achieve this, organizations must implement **robust Access Management systems** that enforce the **principle of least privilege,** enabling users to access only the information and resources necessary for their roles.

A well-designed access management framework provides:

- **Context-aware access intelligence,** enhancing decision-making during access provisioning and monitoring.
- **Improved visibility and auditability** of user activities, helping in early detection of anomalies and potential insider threats.
- **Streamlined controls without operational overhead,** ensuring security does not hinder productivity.
- **Alignment with compliance requirements,** such as ISO 27001, NIST, SOC 2, SEBI Cybersecurity Framework, and regional data protection laws.

By integrating **Identity and Access Management (IAM), Privileged Access Management (PAM),** and **User Access Management (UAM)** into the broader **GRC framework,** organizations can build and sustain a culture of strong **security hygiene,** reducing risk while enabling secure digital operations.

Chapter

8

GRC and Threat Vulnerability Management

1. Introduction

In the digital age, enterprise applications span every layer of business operations - running across on-premises infrastructure and cloud environments alike. These applications are built on diverse platforms, using a mix of development frameworks and operating systems, and are accessible both internally and over the internet.

This dynamic environment is under constant flux: applications are regularly patched or upgraded by internal teams or OEMs, and IT infrastructures are continuously evolving with the addition of new servers, network devices, and security technologies. While this evolution drives innovation and efficiency, it also introduces a critical challenge - **ensuring that each change doesn't create new vulnerabilities.**

Poorly tested updates or misconfigurations can lead to security gaps, unintentionally exposing systems to cybercriminals. These attackers are always on the lookout for weak spots to exploit - whether it's a legacy vulnerability, an unpatched system, or a misconfigured firewall. The result? Disrupted operations, data breaches, reputational damage, and regulatory consequences.

This is where **Threat and Vulnerability Management (TVM)** becomes essential. Embedding a proactive and structured TVM program within your **Information Security Governance framework** ensures that you not only detect and patch vulnerabilities, but also anticipate, evaluate, and mitigate potential risks before they are exploited.

2. Vulnerability Management (VM) Basics

Before diving deeper into how a VM program functions, it's crucial to understand the fundamental differences between three key concepts: **Vulnerability, Threat, and Risk.**

- **Vulnerability**

A Vulnerability is a weakness in the design, code, or configuration of an IT system. It could be the result of a software bug, an overlooked patch, a misconfigured network setting, or even user behavior - such as downloading malicious files. These flaws can be exploited to gain unauthorized access or disrupt operations.

- **Threat**

A Threat is any potential danger or adversarial action that seeks to exploit a vulnerability. This includes cybercriminals using malware, phishing attacks, or zero-day exploits to infiltrate systems and cause damage.

- **Risk**

Risk represents the likelihood of a threat exploiting a vulnerability and the potential impact it may have on the organization. It is essentially the intersection of vulnerability, threat, and consequence - answering the question: "What could go wrong, and how bad would it be?"

To summarize:

A misconfigured application (vulnerability) may be targeted by a ransomware group (threat), creating a **risk** to business continuity and data integrity.

This sets the stage for understanding how a robust **Vulnerability Management** program - aligned with GRC principles - can systematically uncover, prioritize, and address security weaknesses, reducing the organization's overall attack surface.

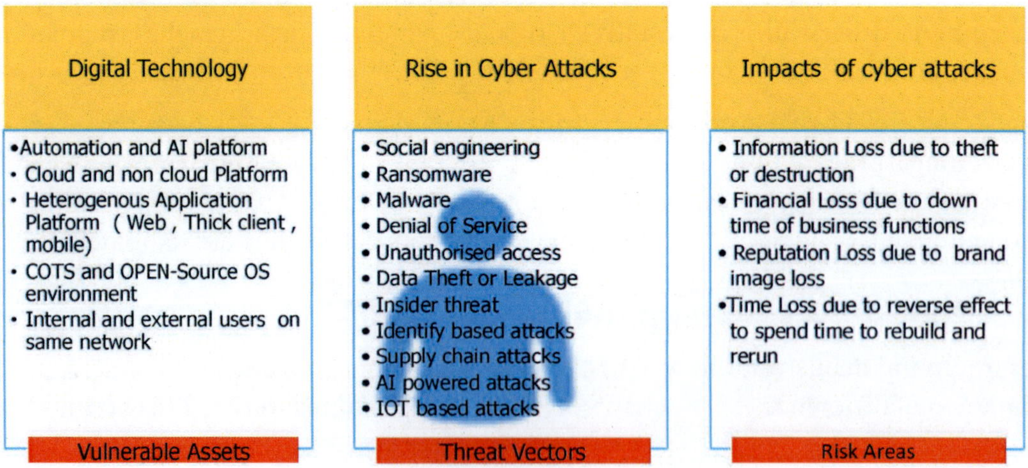

Figure 32 Cyber Attacks and Impacts

3. Vulnerability Management and ISO-OSI reference model

Modern IT infrastructure operates over a complex stack of technologies, often abstracted into the well-known **7 layers of the ISO-OSI (Open Systems Interconnection) model.** Each layer-from physical hardware to application-level protocols-plays a critical role in enabling seamless communication between systems, devices, and applications.

However, **each of these layers can also present unique vulnerabilities,** whether due to configuration flaws, insecure protocols, outdated firmware, or software bugs. As a result, **a comprehensive Vulnerability Management (VM) program must be holistic -** spanning the full breadth of the OSI model to identify and mitigate potential security exposures at every level.

Think of the OSI model as a layered fortress. If even one layer has a weakness, an attacker could breach it - and potentially compromise the entire system.

Below is an illustrative breakdown of how **VM practices map to each OSI layer,** ensuring an end-to-end risk coverage approach:

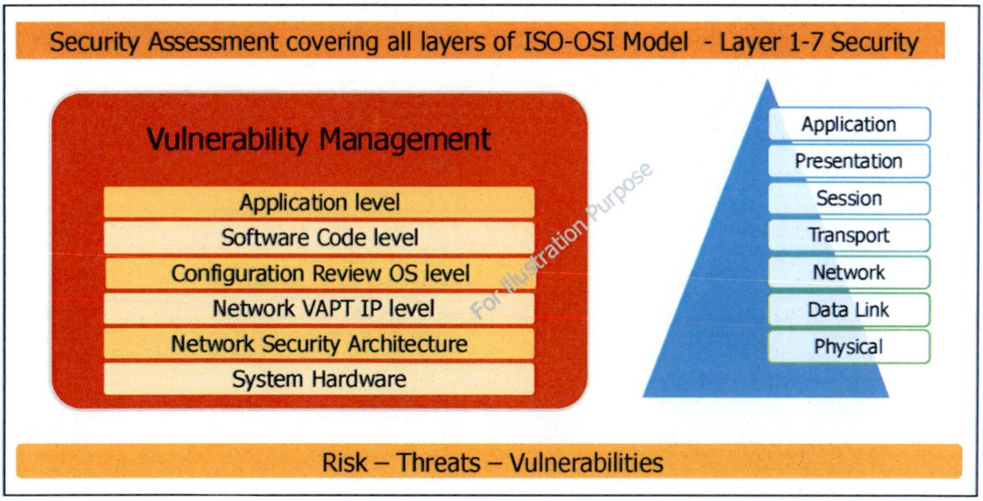

Figure 33 Vulnerability Management Program Model

A Holistic Vulnerability Management (VM) Program

A robust Vulnerability Management (VM) program must operate across **all layers and levels of an organization's IT environment,** whether deployed **on-premises, over intranet,** accessible via the internet, or hosted on **cloud platforms.** Cyber threats don't limit themselves to a specific area-and neither should your vulnerability management strategy.

To achieve true **defense-in-depth,** VM must be aligned with the layered nature of IT infrastructure:

1. **Physical to Data Link Layers (Layers 1–2):**
    - Focus on deployment flaws and technological gaps such as:
        - o Misconfigured LAN/WAN topologies
        - o Hardware vulnerabilities or outdated firmware
        - o IP address-level misallocations or exposure
2. **Network to Session Layers (Layers 3–5):**
    - Address risks stemming from network protocols and communication services, including:
        - o Insecure or exposed IP protocols (e.g., ICMP, UDP, SNMP)
        - o Unnecessary open ports or insecure services
        - o Session management weaknesses (e.g., session fixation, lack of encryption)
3. **Presentation to Application Layers (Layers 6–7):**
    - Mitigate vulnerabilities caused by:
        - o Operating system misconfigurations
        - o Coding flaws in both front-end and back-end applications
        - o Insecure data formatting, handling, or encryption at the presentation layer

Important Note:

Vulnerability Management is a **core technology testing activity.** As part of the GRC (Governance, Risk, and Compliance) framework, it is essential to **understand what each area of the VM program aims to achieve.** However, **the technical implementation details (e.g., scanning techniques, tool configurations)** are beyond the scope of this section.

This approach ensures that your VM strategy is not siloed or limited in scope, but instead, **comprehensively protects the digital assets across all attack surfaces.**

1	Network Security Archiecture	▪ Assessment of the technology posture of the network topology of the organisation ▪ Cyber Security Maturity review with best industry standard practices suh as NIST, C2M2 ▪ High level review of deployment of Perimeter, Content, Communicatoin Security controls ▪ Assessment of deployment of controls such as Access, Backup , log monotoring , Inventory and other at ITGC level
2	Configuration Review	▪ Assessment of Configuration of servers OS,network security applicance with respect to its hardening requirement based on CIS or OEM best practices
3	Network IP VAPT	▪ VA involves scanning of internet / intranet IP address to identify open exposures due to known vulnerbailites and then subsequently demonstrating the exploit which is termed as penetration testing
4	Application Security Testing	▪ Network VAPT is done at IP level , while app security is done at URL / exe level of application . ▪ Testing is done through all the allowable ports in the application or database and Assessemnt is done based OWASP , SANS, Mitre@ttack ▪ The is done across development , testing and production environment
5	Secure Code Review	▪ This involves analyzing an application's source code for security vulnerabilities without the need to execute the code ▪ This approach is commonly used in the software development process to prevent security issues from being introduced in the first place
6	Red Team Exercise	• In context of Vulnerability Assessment and testing it is process through which an organization conduct scenario based testing, using techniques and methods that simulate real-life adversaries • This can be considered as extension of black box testing but test case driven

New Generation Threat and Vulnerability Management (TVM) Platforms – SaaS-Based Services

Beyond traditional Vulnerability Management programs, today's organizations are increasingly adopting **next-generation SaaS-based Threat and Vulnerability Management (TVM) platforms.** These cloud-delivered subscription services offer automation, continuous monitoring, and real-time risk insights-helping organizations rapidly identify vulnerabilities and emerging threats, and enabling faster risk mitigation.

These advanced platforms integrate seamlessly into existing security ecosystems, providing scalable and efficient vulnerability management that adapts to dynamic IT environments.

Some of the cutting-edge technologies and capabilities leveraged by these SaaS-based TVM solutions include:

Attack Surface Management	Ongoing online monitoring the external attack surface perfoming passive, active vulnerability scanning and penetration to identify misconfiguration in applications, servers and other exposed network
Security Risk Scorecard	By aggregating information from various sources, such as web traffic, DNS records and other OSINT data sources, provides a weighted score across various categories / domain components, and insights into detected vulnerabilities.
Dark web and Deep Web monitorng	Get latest threat advisory from Social networking sites, Deep and Dark web including breach credential, breach data, Leak cards, Targeted Frauds, Scams etc
Brand Protection	On going scan of brand / web domain site to helps identify and protect from Impersonation, Phishing, Rogue website, Fake social media accounts, pages, mobile application etc

Each of the above platforms leverages on the new GEN AI technologies and provides high visibitliy into the Threat , Vulnerabilities and Risk with live dasboards and other reports. Many regulatory guidelines have mandated the adoption of the above platform as part if GRC adherance requirements .

Benefits of doing Layered Vulnerability Management Program

- On lines of Defence in depth, layered testing ensures proactive approach and comprehensive testing covering from topology layers to protocol layer to application layer

- Testing at each bottom layer, eliminates false positive at top layer
- Testing at operating system layer, source code level and application layer ensures business logic and use cases are addressed
- A combination of black and gray box testing helps to test the logic at business roles levels, giving granular view of the application, basis which test scenarios can be customised
- Testing a white box level helps to possible identify back door entries left open by developers
- OEM default configurations are not hardened enough at the vanilla deployment state. Configuration review of different devices, servers, database can help iron out gaps developed which might have not addressed at part patching the platform due to oversight
- Network Security topology review for entire application based on ITGC, reviews the application holistically considering perimeter, communication and content security

4. Approach and Methodology for VAPT

This is to give a high-level walk through of what involves in conducting the technical security assessment . Details of the same is not covered as part GRC practical documents.

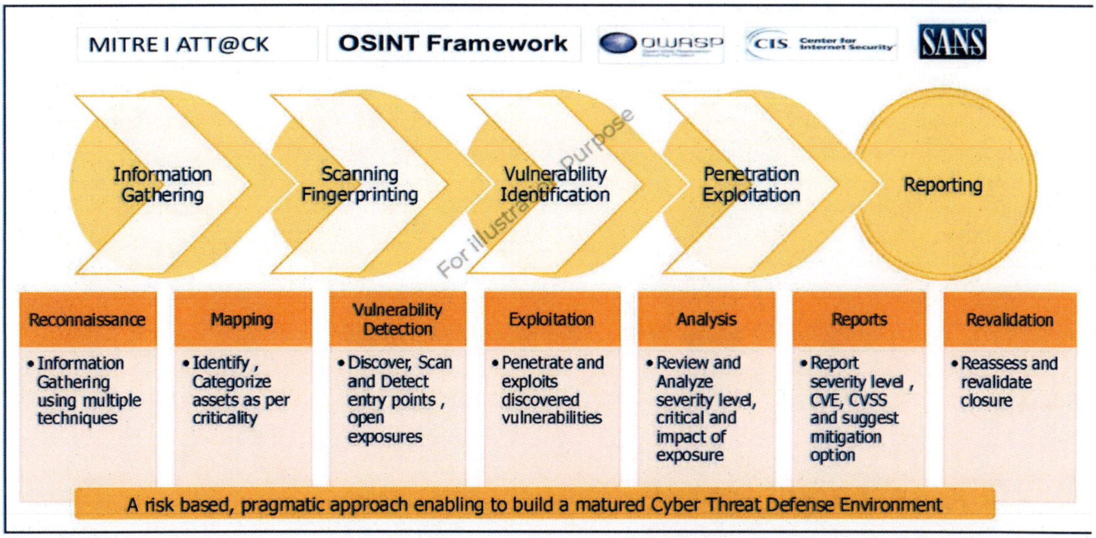

Figure 34 VAPT Workflow for Applications

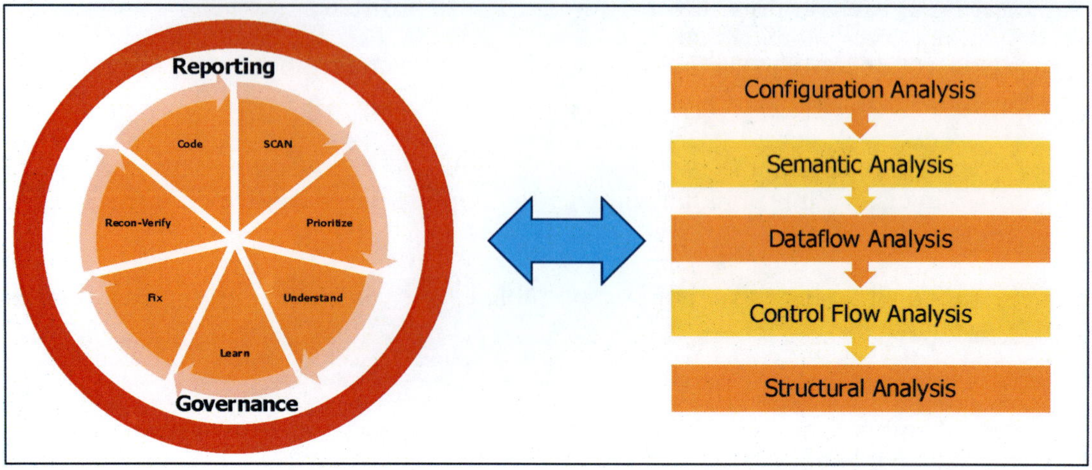

Figure 35 Secure Code Review Approach

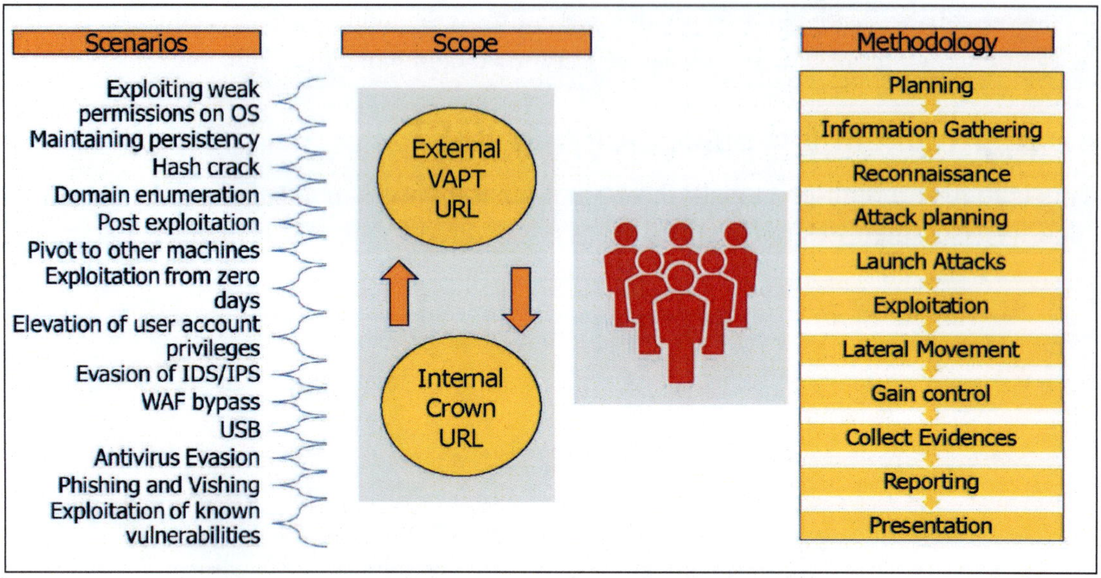

Figure 36 Red Teaming Illustration

(Please note the above schematic are just an indicative approach. Based on the type of environment tests case , business logic needs to be customised and will vary)

5. VM Assessment from GRC perspective

While conducting a VM program review as part of any GRC Audit and Assessment, as an Auditor the program review can be done considering the following

- Understand the network topology with respect to internet / intranet exposure
- Understand the business-critical applications and its usage with in the environment
- Map Network IP, Business applications (internal, external, cloud)
- Review the current calander program (frequency) schedule if available
- Review the current scope of VAPT, Application Security, Configuration Review which has been considered by organisation
- Review the report of VAPT, Application Security and check if they are in lines with Cert-IN or any standard body formats
- Review current status of closure of identified vulnerabilities
- Review the skills of the professionals conducting the test, or fixing the issues
- Review the compliance required for VM program against any defined regulations, standards
- Report observation, recommendations and service improvement program

A customised VM program has to be devised by every organisation, based on attack surface, exposures coverage, locations, number of critical applications, Mobile applications and other parameters. Typical the following can be considered as a practice

External IP	VAPT	Minimum quarterly, both authenticated and non -authenticated
Internal IP	VA	LAN subnet based . The program can be ongoing for large enterprise with a predefined schedule . For SME where not much changes are there, we can consider minimum quarterly
External / Internal Web Applications/ Mobile apps/ Thick clients	DAST	Black box and gray box for every type of user roles. Minimum one time in 3 months. If changes are frequent than as and when required and can be on demand based
All other applications home grown	SAST	On going as part DevSecOps or as part SDLC. With every release or change it has to be done
Servers , Network Security devices	Config review	Minimum quarterly based on OEM best practices and CIS benchmarks

6. Application Security and Secure Application Development Policy Template

Objective:

Protect applications from vulnerabilities throughout their lifecycle by embedding security measures in every stage of the application development process, from design to deployment, and continuously assessing their security posture

1. Scope

This policy applies to:

- All software applications developed, deployed, or used by the organization
- The entire Software Development Life Cycle (SDLC), including planning, design, development, testing, deployment, and maintenance phases
- Both in-house developed applications and third-party applications integrated into the organization's systems

2. Policy Statements

2.1. Integrate Security in the Software Development Life Cycle (SDLC)

- **Objective:** Ensure that security is integrated into the SDLC from the initial design phase to final deployment, reducing vulnerabilities and risks in the application
- **Key Controls:**
    - **Security by Design:** Incorporate security requirements into the application's design phase. Identify potential risks and threats early in the planning stages to build secure solutions from the ground up.
    - **Threat Modeling:** Conduct threat modeling during the design phase to identify security risks and potential attack vectors. This should involve both technical and non-technical stakeholders, including developers, architects, and business leaders.
    - **Security Reviews:** Conduct Security Reviews and Risk Assessments at each phase of the SDLC, including code reviews, design reviews, and testing. Ensure that security is not an afterthought, but a core component throughout the lifecycle.

  - **Agile and DevSecOps:** Implement security practices within Agile and DevSecOps workflows to ensure continuous integration and continuous delivery (CI/CD) pipelines are secure, with automated security testing and vulnerability scanning integrated into the development process.

2.2. Perform Vulnerability Assessments and Penetration Tests (VAPT)

- **Objective:** Continuously assess and identify security vulnerabilities within applications to mitigate risks before deployment and throughout the application's lifecycle
- **Key Controls:**
  - **Vulnerability Scanning:** Regularly scan applications and their underlying infrastructure for known vulnerabilities using automated tools and manual testing. This should be done before deployment and periodically during the application's lifecycle
  - **Penetration Testing (Pen Testing):** Conduct penetration testing on applications to identify potential vulnerabilities that could be exploited by attackers. Ensure that tests cover both functional and non-functional security aspects, such as authentication, authorization, input validation, and error handling
  - **Third-Party Assessments:** Include third-party application security testing for any externally sourced or integrated applications, ensuring that external dependencies do not introduce additional risks

2.3. Enforce Secure Coding Practices and Third-Party Library Scans

- **Objective:** Mitigate risks by ensuring that coding practices adhere to secure programming standards and by identifying and managing the security risks associated with third-party libraries
- **Key Controls:**
  - **Secure Coding Standards:** Enforce secure coding practices that align with industry standards, such as OWASP Top 10 and SANS Secure Coding Guidelines
  - Developers must be trained on secure coding practices to avoid introducing vulnerabilities like SQL injection, Cross-Site Scripting (XSS), and Cross-Site Request Forgery (CSRF)

- **Code Analysis Tools:** Integrate automated code analysis tools within the CI/CD pipeline to identify and fix common vulnerabilities during the development process. These tools should scan for both static (source code) and dynamic (running application) vulnerabilities
- **Input Validation:** Ensure all user inputs are validated, sanitized, and filtered to prevent injection attacks, data manipulation, and unauthorized access
- **Dependency and Library Scanning:** Regularly scan third-party libraries, open-source components, and dependencies used in applications for known vulnerabilities ,using tools like OWASP Dependency-Check, Snyk, or similar solutions to automate this process
- **Patch Management for Libraries:** Implement a patch management process to ensure that all third-party libraries are updated and patched for security vulnerabilities in a timely manner

2.4. Application Security Testing

- **Objective:** Implement thorough testing mechanisms to identify and address security weaknesses before applications are deployed or updated
- **Key Controls:**
  - **Static Application Security Testing (SAST):** Perform static analysis of source code to detect vulnerabilities during development. SAST tools analyze the code for security flaws before it is executed, ensuring vulnerabilities are identified early
  - **Dynamic Application Security Testing (DAST):** Use DAST to test running applications for vulnerabilities that can only be detected during execution, such as misconfigurations, session management issues, and vulnerabilities introduced through the network
  - **Interactive Application Security Testing (IAST):** Use IAST tools during manual testing to identify vulnerabilities as the application runs, providing more detailed insights and reducing the number of false positives

2.5. Security in Deployment and Maintenance

- **Objective:** Ensure secure deployment and ongoing maintenance of applications, addressing vulnerabilities that may emerge after deployment

- **Key Controls:**
    - o **Secure Deployment Practices:** Use secure deployment practices, including encrypting sensitive data during transmission and ensuring proper access controls during the deployment process
    - o **Post-Deployment Monitoring:** Continuously monitor applications after deployment for any unusual activity or vulnerabilities that may surface.
    - o Use application performance monitoring (APM) tools to detect anomalies, and integrate these with security information and event management (SIEM) tools
    - o **Patch Management:** Continuously update and patch applications after deployment to fix any newly discovered vulnerabilities and maintain an up-to-date inventory of all patches and their associated risk mitigations
    - o **Secure Configuration Management:** Ensure that all application configurations, including network, database, and user access settings, are properly hardened according to security best practices and are regularly reviewed

2.6. Roles and Responsibilities

- **Development Team:** Responsible for integrating security throughout the SDLC, adhering to secure coding standards, and ensuring that the application is tested for vulnerabilities
- **Security Team:** Oversee security assessments such as vulnerability scanning, penetration testing, and code reviews and ensure that security tools are integrated into the development process
- **Quality Assurance (QA) Team:** Test the application for functionality, usability, and security by collaborating with the development and security teams and ensure that security testing is included in the overall test plan
- **IT Operations Team:** Manage the deployment, maintenance, and patching of applications, ensuring that all security measures are maintained in live environments
- **Compliance and Audit Team:** Ensure that all security requirements related to application security are met, and periodically review and audit the application security controls

7. Conclusion

Whether conducted through traditional manual testing with tools or leveraging new-generation AI-powered solutions, **Vulnerability Management remains a cornerstone of any effective GRC program.** It enables organizations to proactively identify and address potential threat vectors arising from known vulnerabilities-before cybercriminals can exploit them.

Failing to manage these vulnerabilities can lead to severe consequences, including operational disruptions, data breaches, financial losses, and lasting damage to brand reputation. Recognized as a mandatory requirement across all major security standards and frameworks, a well-established Vulnerability Management program ensures continuous risk monitoring and threat mitigation-empowering organizations to stay resilient in an ever-evolving threat landscape.

Chapter

9

GRC and IT-OT Assessment

1. Introduction

Industrial Automation and Control Systems (IACS) form the backbone of critical infrastructure sectors such as manufacturing, power generation, nuclear plants, pharmaceuticals, water utilities, oil and natural gas industries, and service providers. Cyber attacks targeting these mission-critical systems pose severe risks-not only to operational continuity, but also to the safety of field personnel, the environment, social services, financial stability, and even national security.

To counter these evolving threats, organizations must adopt a proactive, ongoing approach to **identify, detect, prevent, mitigate, respond to, and recover from cyber incidents** within these complex environments.

Modern IACS environments are a fusion of legacy SCADA and process control systems combined with new-generation IT, IIoT (Industrial Internet of Things), and OT (Operational Technology) smart systems. Managing this multi-tiered, multi-protocol, multi-vendor, and heterogeneous IT-IIoT-OT ecosystem requires a **comprehensive and robust Governance, Risk, and Compliance (GRC) framework** integrated with Information System Security controls. This framework enables continuous real-time monitoring and protection of critical assets from an ever-expanding landscape of cyber threats.

2. IACS IT-OT Network Overview

The IT-OT ecosystem operates over a complex, multi-tiered converged network. This network runs on a mix of standardized IP protocols and proprietary, OEM-specific communication standards. Industries such as Energy, Water, Oil & Gas, Electricity, Traffic Control, Manufacturing, and Engineering all rely on ICS (Industrial Control Systems) for their operations.

Below is a high-level schematic illustrating the layered topology typical of an integrated IT and OT network environment.

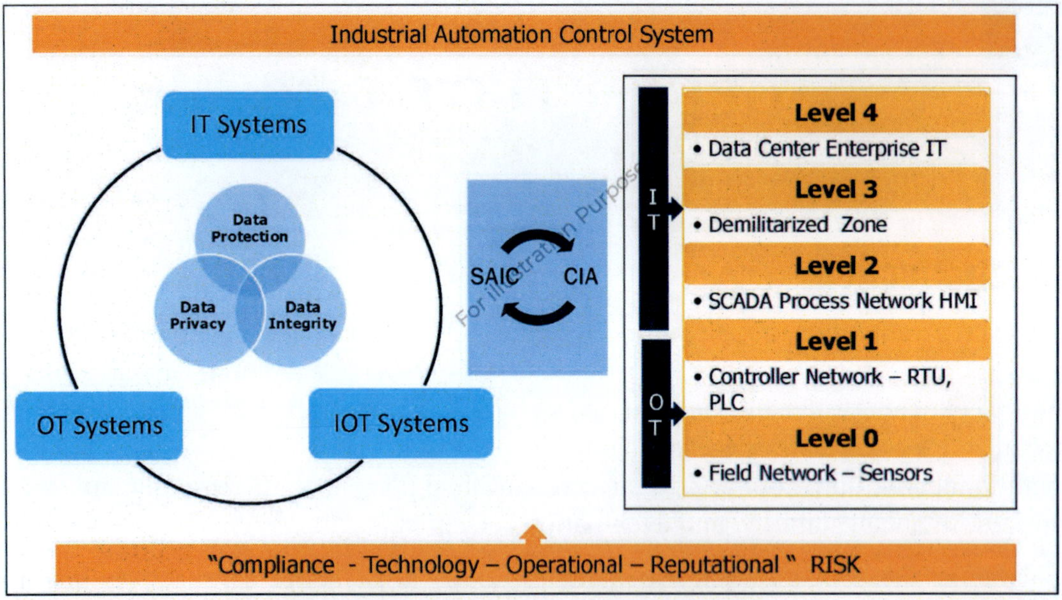

Figure 37 IT- OT Layers Representation

Industrial Control Systems (ICS) are intricate ecosystems where numerous individual components are seamlessly integrated to achieve the operational and process objectives of a plant or facility. These components collectively function across Level 0 to Level 3 of the ICS network architecture and encompass a variety of specialized control systems, including but not limited to:

- Supervisory Control and Data Acquisition (SCADA) - is a category of industrial control systems (ICS) that remotely gathers data in real time from industrial processes in order to supervise and control equipment and conditions. It controls and monitors industrial devices, and make data-driven decisions regarding their industrial processes.
- Distributed Control System (DCS) - are built using sensors and controllers to acquire and process data. The sensors then connect to a centralized hub for processing and generating actionable outputs.
- Programmable Logical Computer (PLC) - These tiny computers use basic input-output functions to operate. Their main role is to control the system's functions using their internal logic. PLCs rely on OT technology to work correctly.

- Human machine interfaces (HMI) - A user interface must be connected to a machine or system so humans can operate the device. Most HMIs have PLCs built into them.
- Remote Terminal Units (RTU) - interface with field devices such as sensors, actuators and valves to collect raw telemetry data and transform it into useful information for human consumption.
- Sensors / Actuators are typical field devices which collects inputs from various specific process and send the current status back to SCADA.

Each level within the IT-OT environment serves a distinct function, which can generally be described as follows:

- **Levels 0 to 2:** Primarily consist of the SCADA network and its associated systems. These levels control and monitor the physical processes and are typically replicated across all operational locations to ensure consistency and reliability.
- **Level 3:** Acts as a crucial separation layer, serving as a demilitarized zone (DMZ) or barrier between core OT components and the IT systems. The design of WAN and LAN connectivity between locations varies depending on the industry-specific technologies in use.
- **Level 4:** Focuses on business operations, hosting Management Information Systems (MIS) and other enterprise applications that support decision-making and overall organizational functions.

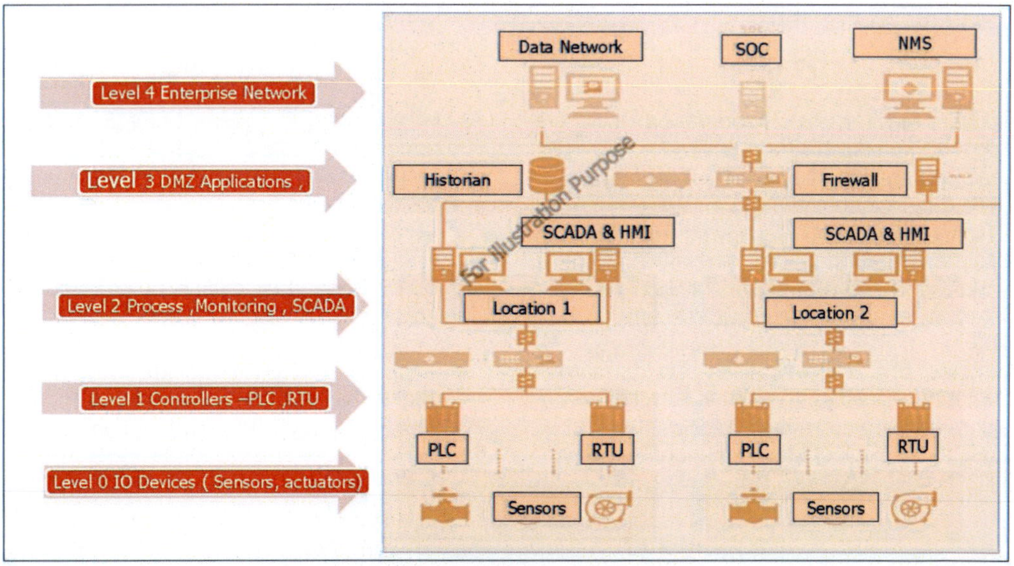

Figure 38 OT Network Layers

3. GRC in IT-OT Environment

Industrial Control Systems (ICS) are now increasingly exposed to the same range of cyber threats that affect traditional IT environments. However, the consequences of a breach in ICS are often far more severe-ranging from physical damage and production outages to serious safety hazards. The growing use of wireless technologies, mobile devices, and automated systems across both IT and OT environments has significantly expanded the attack surface. What was once limited to business-level threats (Level 4) now affects critical operational layers such as Level 0 and Level 1.

Given the high-stakes nature of IACS operations, **Governance, Risk, and Compliance (GRC)** must be integrated holistically-across **security, safety, and surveillance** functions. However, the priority focus varies between IT and OT layers:

- In **IT environments,** the emphasis is on Confidentiality, Integrity, and Availability (C-I-A).
- In **OT environments,** the priority shifts toward **Safety, Availability, Integrity, and then Confidentiality (S-A-I-C)**-reflecting the operational imperative to protect human lives, maintain continuous industrial processes, and ensure the integrity of physical systems.

Implementing a structured GRC framework helps ensure that threat identification, control measures, and response capabilities are timely, effective, and aligned with both IT and OT operational goals. The figure below provides details on the ICS vulnerabilities and associated threats .

ICS vulnerabilities

- Exposure to Internet (ICS operation exposed to public environment)
- Weak Segregation of IT – OT (Integration needs due to automation)
- Default Configuration (legacy system obsolete Operating system, firmware)
- Weakness in ICS protocols (traditional system were not designed with security in mind)
- Weakness of ICS applications (non standard development leading to open vulnerabilities)
- Lack of security awareness (social engineering , lack of knowledge on field on digital technologies)

ICS Threats

- Malware threats (portable platform, removable media on field , Phishing in social media)
- Insider attacks (malpractice by internal users intentionally / non intentionally , disgruntled employees)
- Denial of Service (hackers, crackers)
- Third Party Threats (access to vendors, OEM)
- Technical or physical malfunction , operational level errors, technical breakdown
- Threats for terrorists (nation state actors)

Figure 39 ICS Vulnerabilities and Threats

While considering doing a Risk Assessment or Compliance Review for an industry which uses both IT and OT infrastructure in its process needs, it is required to adopt an integrated approach considering multiple standards and regulations and include:

- ISO27001:2022 – Implementation of Information Security Management System
- ISA / IEC 62443 - The International Society of Automation (ISA) and the International Electrotechnical Commission (IEC) have joined forces to address the need to improve the cybersecurity of IACS
- NIST CSF – IT Cybersecurity; NIST 800-82 – OT Cybersecurity, NIST 800-53 – For OT Reference
- NCIIPC - National Critical Information Infrastructure Protection a unit of NTRO guidelines
- IT General Controls aligned to ITIL framework
- Service Organization Controls (SOC) 2 audit examines your organization's controls are in place that protect and secure its system or services used by customers or partners.
- Digital Personal Data Protection Act on privacy
- Industry specific requirement such as NERC for Power, 21 CFR part 11 for pharma, CPS and Industry 4.0 specific as applicable
- ISO42001 – Artificial Intelligence Management System in case of using AI Environment for development

Details of above standards and guidelines is out of the scope of this section and names are used for giving a generic understanding.

4. Assessment Approach

Auditing or Assessing an IT-OT converged environment is inherently complex due to the blend of legacy systems, proprietary protocols, and modern IT technologies. To ensure the assessment is effective and aligned with organizational objectives, the process must begin with clear scoping and boundary definition.

As part of the **initial information-gathering phase,** it is essential to collect key foundational data that will shape the scope, depth, and direction of the assessment. This includes:

- **Understanding the business and operational context:** Identify the critical functions and processes supported by the IT-OT infrastructure
- **Mapping the physical and logical architecture:** Document the network layout, communication flows, devices, and protocols across IT and OT layers
- **Identifying critical assets and interdependencies:** Highlight systems, devices, and applications that are essential for both operational continuity and security
- **Reviewing existing cybersecurity practices:** Evaluate the current state of security controls, monitoring tools, and incident response capabilities
- **Assessing compliance drivers:** Determine applicable standards and regulations (e.g., ISA/IEC 62443, NIST 800-82, ISO 27001) guiding the security posture

By establishing a strong foundation during the discovery phase, organizations can size the audit scope appropriately and tailor the assessment methodology to address unique challenges inherent in IT-OT environments.

SN	Some question to consider while sizing
1	How many number and location of sites to cover under IT-OT
2	Is IT and OT locations in same environment or different
3	What are types of protocols used in both IT and OT
4	What is current ecosystem of OT i.e. OEM , platform, SCADA , PLC, HMI, Historian
5	Do you have functional and process documentation for IACS
6	How many number and types of IT applications for IT environment
7	How many numbers and types of IT applications supporting OT
8	Is ICS centralised of distributed
9	Have you deployed any AI-ML based automation
10	Are you using cloud for any of the components in ICS
11	Does you OT environment use any mobile, wireless technology at lower level i.e. 0,1,2
12	What is current ICS monitoring process for SOC , NOC
13	Have you conducted any risk assessment before
14	Is you IT/OT environment managed inhouse or outsourced

Figure 40 IT-OT Information Gathering Template

The above list is an indicative and not comprehensive. Based on each type of OT environment i.e. Power, Water, Energy, Telcom the type of equipment varies, based on whether it is for generation, distribution, transmission, manufacturing, or retail environment. An organization considering to adopt a standard or guidelines should look at doing a pilot project for few sites, roll out the implementation and then post stability can expand the scope in phases across all locations.

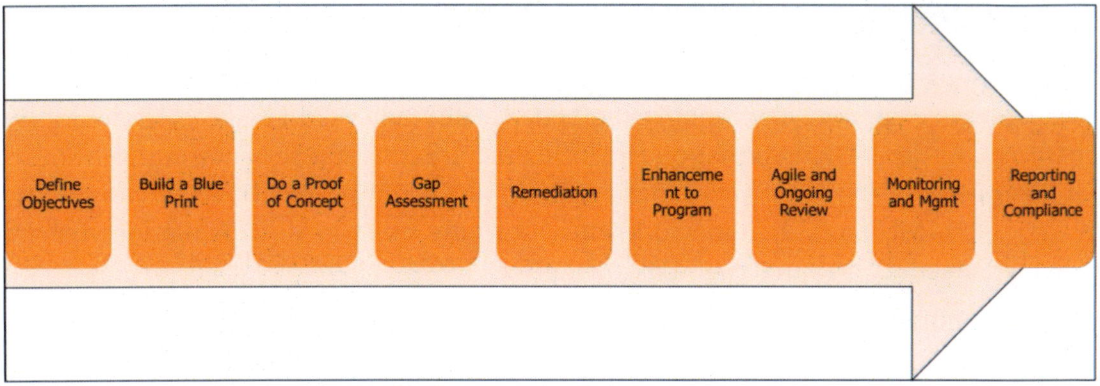

Figure 41 Indicative Audit Workflow

The above approach can be further granularly broken in tracks covering different aspect of specific to IT , OT , Applications, VM and other areas. An indicative approach is presented below which can be used as reference.

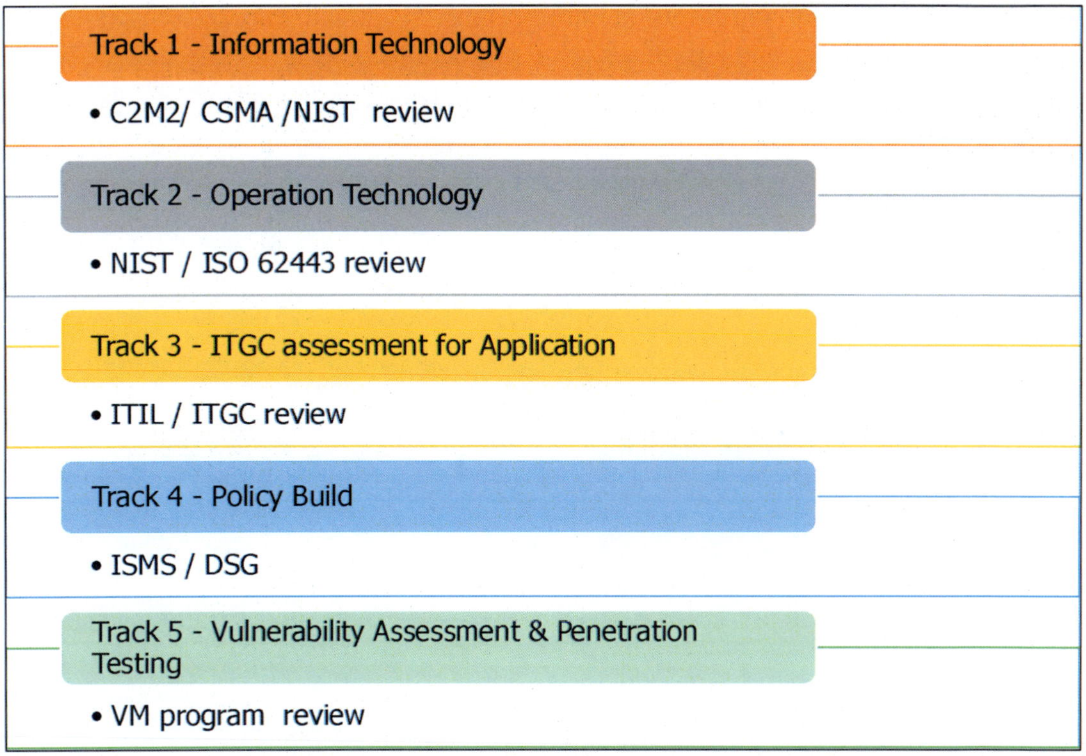

Figure 42 IACS Assessment Tracks for illustration

5. Conclusion

Organizations leveraging OT technologies often operate with a significant footprint of legacy systems, now increasingly integrated with traditional IT and modern digital platforms. As digital transformation and infrastructure convergence accelerate, the need for a **robust and dynamic Governance, Risk, and Compliance (GRC) framework** becomes critical. Such a framework must not only exist in documentation, but be actively embedded within day-to-day operations.

Given the multifaceted nature of these environments-and the growing list of regulatory and compliance obligations-a **centralized, managed GRC platform** becomes a strategic necessity. This platform should offer seamless integration with the organization's existing technology stack, enabling real-time visibility, compliance tracking, and risk mitigation.

An effective Vulnerability Management (VM) program, tailored to the **layered IT-OT network model,** must span all tiers-from business applications to field-level control systems. Proactive detection of early warning signals requires placing **network discovery and monitoring tools** at appropriate layers, customized based on the underlying technologies and communication protocols in use.

In the next section, we will explore how **Contextual Security Intelligence (CSI)** can empower organizations to enhance their threat detection, security monitoring, and decision-making processes-enabling a smarter, risk-aware operational environment.

Chapter

10

GRC and Event and Log Management

1. Introduction

Virtually every system process generates some form of logging data. Managing and monitoring logs across systems, applications, servers, network devices, and user activities is inherently complex-yet crucial. Logs serve as a vital component of system intelligence, offering insights into current operations, historical activities, and potential issues such as data anomalies, unauthorized access, or performance degradation.

Traditionally, logs were primarily used for system diagnostics. However, in today's fully IT-enabled business environment, **centralized log collection and storage** is essential-not only for troubleshooting but also for compliance, auditing, incident investigation, and cybersecurity.

As part of a **robust GRC framework,** it is critical to identify all **key infrastructure assets and applications,** and embed **log collection, storage, and monitoring** mechanisms right from the design stage to support continuous risk management and governance objectives.

2. Benefits of Logging

Logs can be broadly categorized into two primary types:

- **System/Operational Logs (Machine-Generated):**

  These include logs that report on system health and status, such as:

  - Performance warnings
  - Hardware/software errors
  - SNMP traps
  - Resource malfunctions

- **Security/Activity Logs (User/Network-Generated):**

  These include logs that provide visibility into security posture and access activities, such as:

  - User access logs
  - Activity monitoring logs
  - Firewall and threat detection logs
  - Policy usage reports
  - Network traffic logs

Most modern devices and applications generate logs in standardized formats such as Syslog, making it easier to parse and centralize data using Security Information and Event Management (SIEM) tools.

When integrated with **Contextual Security Intelligence (CSI)** and automation, log monitoring becomes a strategic enabler of **predictive threat management** and risk-based decision-making. This shifts the organization from a reactive security posture to a proactive and eventually predictive one.

Automated Log Monitoring supports the GRC framework by:

- Monitoring, Reviewing and Auditing Operational data ,leading to increased transparency
- Track administrators, service providers and OEM activities across IT assets
- Track security events generated from various resources and generate alerts and early warning signals
- Reduce risks against loss and theft of electronic data due to internal threats and APT attacks
- Trending log data which helps to understand usage, and operational behavior of the IT assets
- Enables adherence to IT policy enforcement and compliance to standards
- Assists in doing digital incident and forensic response

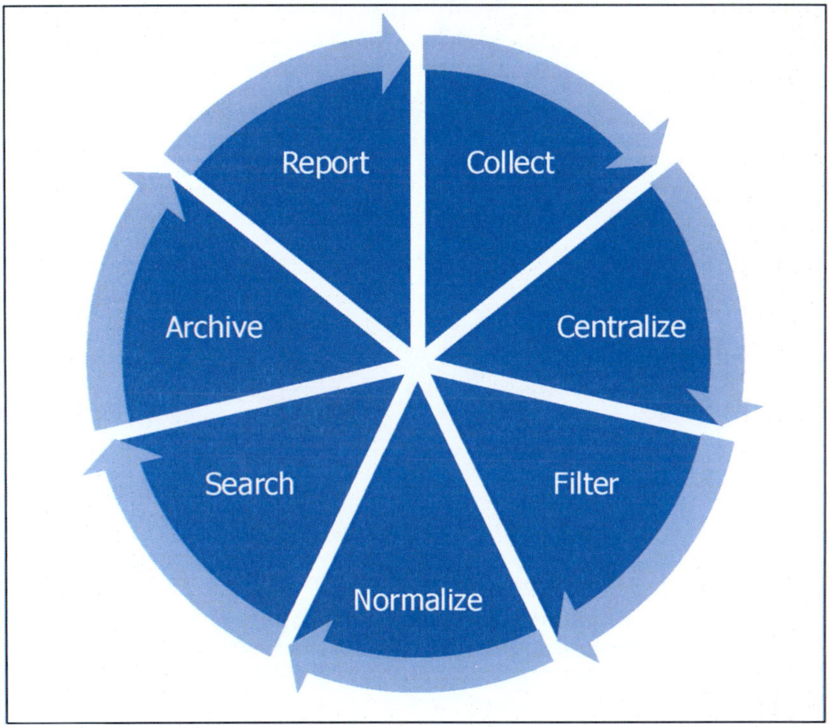

Figure 43 Log Management Workflow

3. Event and Log Management – Contextual Based Security Intelligence

In modern security architecture, **Event and Log Management** is no longer limited to basic log aggregation. Instead, it is driven by **contextual intelligence** to help organizations proactively detect, analyze, and respond to threats in a timely manner.

Contemporary cybersecurity tools come in various forms, each with integrated log collection capabilities. These include:

- **SIEM** (Security Information and Event Management)
- **UEBA** (User and Entity Behavior Analytics)
- **EDR** (Endpoint Detection and Response)
- **XDR** (Extended Detection and Response)
- **DLP** (Data Loss Prevention)
- **Threat Intelligence Platforms**

These tools collect logs and events generated from a wide variety of systems, devices, applications, and user activities. Events generated due to various activities performed on different devices are collected as logs , are forwarded to central collectors, which are analysed (manual or automated) and converted in Alerts or Alarms .

Based on the criticality and post removal of any false positive, for critical alerts incident tickets are raised, which are then addressed by respective resolver teams . The typical life cycle of event while it is generated and converted to an incidents is shown below:

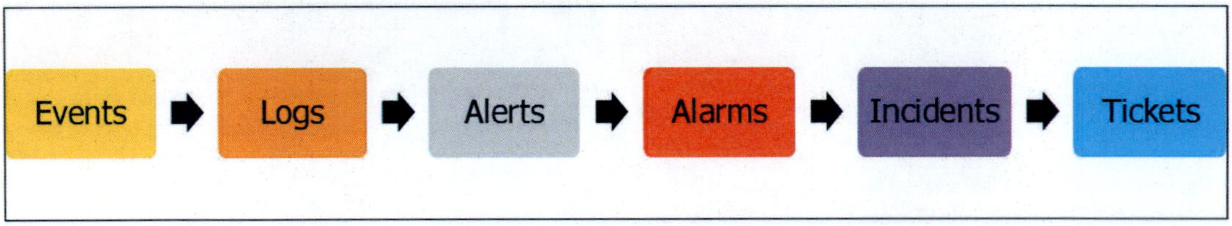

Figure 44 Event Log Cycle

The log collectors based on the solution and platform can be implemented or integrated with the IT environment at different locations, and be used for:

- Centralized Collection and normalization of audit data from various sources in a defined format
- Filtering auditing data based on warning, critical, information type events
- Classifying data based on priority and criticality
- Trending and reporting statistical information of the various events
- Storing logs (online and offline) as per retention period defined
- Build correlation tool basis which event can be converted into alerts and subsequent Tickets
- End User logs can be used for user entity behaviors analysis
- Fusing Threat Intelligence data from different feeds and using AL-ML can be used for threat detection

4. Security Operation Center - A view Point

Log monitoring and management has become a **near-mandatory requirement under various regulatory and compliance frameworks** (e.g., ISO 27001, NIST, NCIIPC, SEBI-CSCRF, PCI DSS, and others). It plays a critical role in ensuring visibility, traceability, and accountability across the digital ecosystem.

The **Security Operations Centre (SOC)** forms the nerve center for cybersecurity monitoring. Its core function revolves around delivering **context-driven security intelligence** based on logs and telemetry data, offering a proactive and predictive mechanism to:

- Detect anomalies early
- Identify emerging threats
- Prevent and respond to cyberattacks in a timely manner
- Mitigate potential risks before they escalate

The schematic below shows a view point of providing "Proactive and Predictive" Threat Intelligence and Analysis by leveraging inputs and logs data from multiple tools .

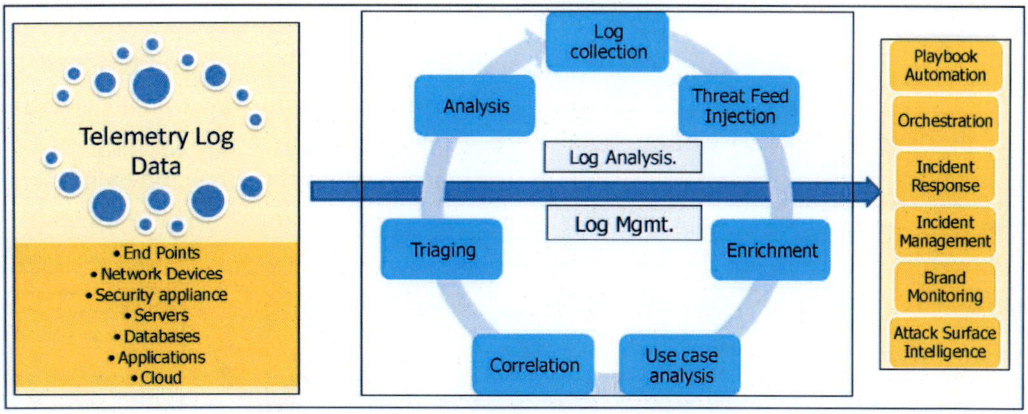

Figure 45 Log Management and Monitoring

Centralized Telemetry and Threat Intelligence Fusion

Logs and telemetry data are sourced from multiple layers of the IT-OT-IIoT environment, including but not limited to:

- Endpoints
- Servers
- Firewalls
- SCADA/ICS Devices
- Network Infrastructure
- Cloud Platforms
- Identity and Access Management systems
- Application and Database Servers

This **heterogeneous telemetry data** is **collected centrally** into platforms such as SIEM, XDR, or a Data Lake. These logs are then **fused with external and internal threat intelligence feeds** (e.g., from ISACs, CERTs, commercial threat intel platforms). Post ingestion, the system performs:

- **Enrichment** with contextual metadata (e.g., asset criticality, location, known vulnerabilities)
- **Triaging and Correlation and behavior analysis** using next-generation AI/ML models
- **Generation of risk-prioritized alerts or incident tickets**
- **Triggering of automated response workflows** through Security Orchestration, Automation, and Response (SOAR)

Details of different tools is out of the scope of this document. The concept has been used to demonstrate how a structured GRC approach plays an important role in building a Cyber Vigilant and Cyber Resilient operational framework. The workflow shown below is to give an illustration of Security operations Incident monitoring and management function

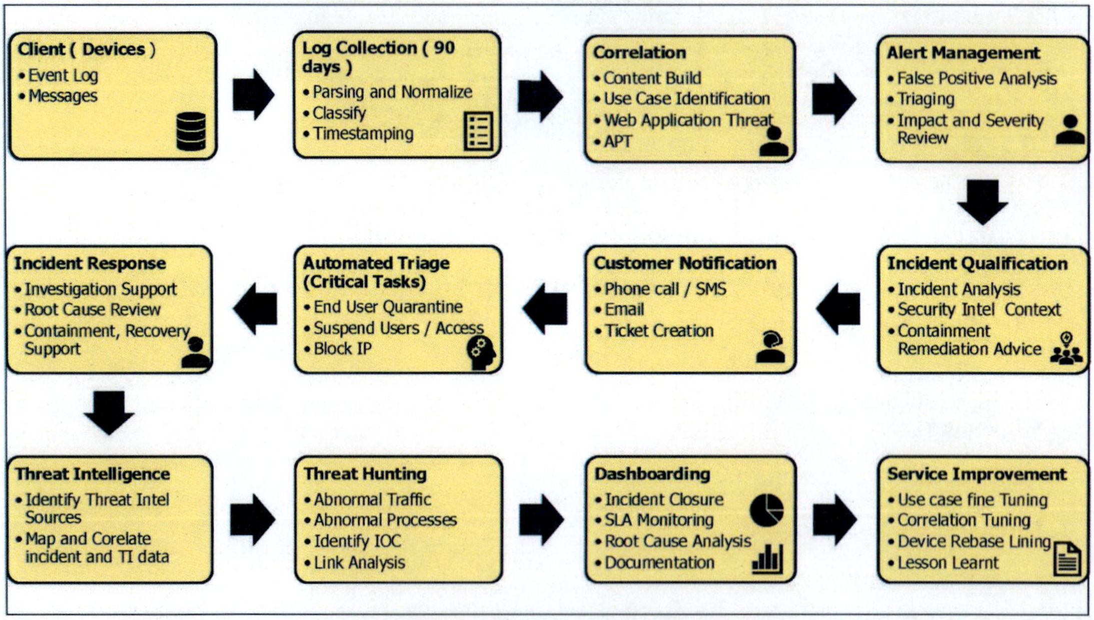

Figure 46 Incident Management Workflow

SOC environment, associated tools and services when mapped to NIST layers can be viewed as below:

Identify and Detect	Prevent and Protect	Respond and Recover
Event Monitoring	Incident and Event Management(SIEM)	Orchestration and Automation
Threat Intelligence Monitoring	Extended Detection and Response (XDR)	Incident Response & Forensics
Log Monitoring and Management	Network Packet Flows and Attack Path Analysis	Malware - Ransomware Analysis
User Entity Behavior	Dark Web monitoring	Brand Reputation monitoring
AI/ML Driven Threat Hunting	Attack Surface Intelligence	

Figure 47 NIST Mapping SOC Services for illustration

5. Risk Assessments for Security Operation

A Risk Assessment of Organization's Security Operations with respect to its applicability, its criticality and its adherence to regulatory requirement should be done as part of building the operational framework. The following questions can be considered as part of Risk Assessment

- Is compliance with adopted standards and regulation a mandatory requirement
- Have you carried out the Risk Assessment of your IT assets and business application to determine the risk exposure and threats
- How you identified which device / application logs will be required to be collected
- Is any type of log data collected in any manner
- Do you think there is threat towards data leakage and data theft from internal users
- What is the current maturity level with respect to security operations
- What are the organization KPI's, dashboard requirements to measure operational risks, threats and security events
- How is the current IT and operations managed
- Do you have dedicated Network and Security Administration team

6. Conclusion

A comprehensive, well-scoped risk assessment enables to build, design and operationalize a Security Operations Centre that is **aligned with organizational priorities, threat exposure, and regulatory needs.** It ensures the GRC framework is supported by **measurable, responsive, and resilient security operations.**

Chapter

11

GRC and Cyber Crisis Management Plan

1. Introduction

In today's hyperconnected world, every organization - from manufacturers to financial institutions - is only one click away from a potential cyber crisis. As digital transformation accelerates, so too does the sophistication and frequency of cyber threats. What once took attackers weeks to plan can now be executed in minutes, thanks to advanced tools, automation, and even **AI-driven attack kits** readily available on the dark web.

A cyber-attack today is no longer just an IT issue - it's a **business crisis.** It can paralyze operations, erode stakeholder trust, trigger regulatory scrutiny, and damage the very foundation of a brand. In such a high-stakes environment, **being unprepared is not an option.**

Enter the **Cyber Crisis Management Plan (CCMP)** - your organization's digital firefighting blueprint.

A CCMP isn't just a document. It's a **battle-tested game plan** that unites your technical teams, leadership, communications, legal, and compliance stakeholders under one clear objective: **Respond fast. Recover smarter. Restore trust.**

Why Every Organization Needs a CCMP

Imagine this: Your SOC detects unusual outbound traffic from a critical server. Within minutes, customer data is exfiltrated, systems go offline, and media outlets begin to report the incident. Without a crisis plan, chaos ensues - who responds? Who informs the regulator? How do you contain the attack?

Now imagine the same scenario with a CCMP in place:

- Your incident response team swings into action
- Business continuity protocols isolate affected systems

- Communications teams inform stakeholders with accuracy and confidence
- Regulatory notifications are made within required timelines
- Most importantly, the damage is contained and recovery begins - with your brand reputation intact

The New Threat Landscape

Today's attackers are faster, smarter, and more unpredictable. They don't just go after your servers - they target your cloud apps, your third-party vendors, your employees' mobile devices, and even your OT environments. And they're not alone - AI is helping them find cracks in your defenses faster than ever.

With IT assets spread across on-prem, cloud, SaaS, and hybrid environments, the attack surface is wider than ever. And while AI brings incredible benefits to defenders, it also arms bad actors with tools that shorten the attack cycle and increase the impact radius.

The result? A cyber crisis can escalate in seconds - and that's why you need a CCMP ready to activate before the breach becomes breaking news.

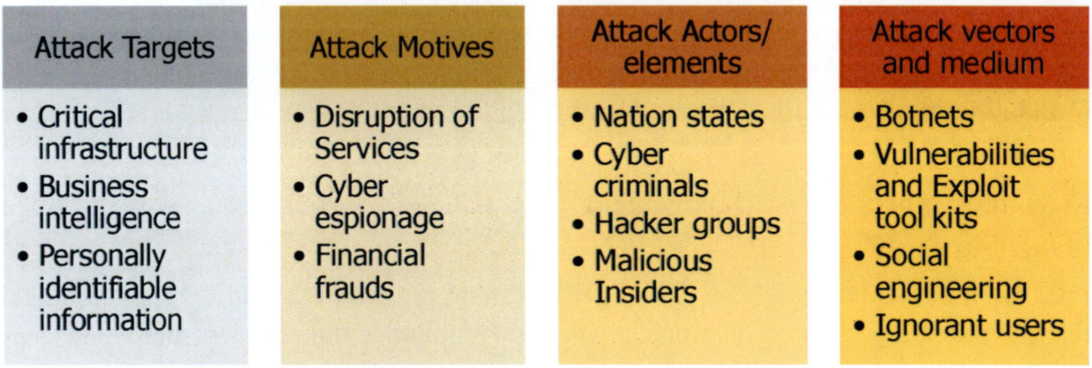

Figure 48 Cyber Threat Landscape

2. Cyber Incident Management

Cyber incidents are no longer a matter of "if" - they are a matter of "when". Whether it's a ransomware outbreak, data breach, system compromise, or a major DDoS attack, incidents can **cripple operations, disrupt critical services,** and cause significant **financial and reputational loss.**

What is a Cyber Incident?

By definition, a **cyber incident** refers to any activity - malicious or accidental - that disrupts the **confidentiality, integrity, or availability (CIA)** of information systems or data. These incidents may stem from cyber-attacks, internal malfunctions, human errors, or third-party compromises.

The **impact** can range from a minor glitch in one server to a **business-wide outage.** Hence, incidents are usually classified into **four severity levels:**

- **Critical** – Catastrophic impact; immediate executive involvement required
- **High** – Significant operational disruption; fast-track response needed
- **Medium** – Limited impact on business; localized containment possible
- **Low** – Minor incident; routine handling

Why Incident Management Matters?

In the face of escalating threats, having a well-defined **Cyber Incident Management Plan (CIMP)** becomes not just important, but essential. This plan enables organizations to:

- **Detect incidents early** through proper monitoring and threat intelligence
- **Contain and mitigate** the damage quickly to prevent lateral spread
- **Recover operations** in a structured and timely manner
- **Analyze root causes** to avoid recurrence
- **Communicate effectively** with stakeholders and regulators

Key Phases in Cyber Incident Management

The incident management lifecycle can be divided into the following high-level phases, each with supporting sub-activities:

- **Incident Detection:** Identify / Detect / Report Incident, Define and take Ownership, Validate and Verification of Incident, Obtain and gather Incident Details, Log Incident Details and raise an Incident Tickets as per IT Service Management requirements
- **Incident Classification:** Analyze, Triage, Define & Assign Type i.e. severity, Category and Priority as per impact , Provide Initial Support, Allocate Incident
- **Investigation and Diagnosis:** Take Technical Ownership, Ensure Correct Assignment, Initial Client Contact, Match Incident, Investigate Incident & Diagnose Incident, Update Incident Details, Functional Escalation
- **Resolution and Recovery:** Implement solution / workaround, Ensure Recovery, Record solution
- **Incident Closure:** Confirm Closure, Admin and Quality, Close Incident

Objective of the Incident Management Process

The **primary goal of Incident Management** is to ensure that any disruption to IT services is resolved as quickly and efficiently as possible - minimizing impact on business operations and restoring normalcy within agreed **Service Level Agreements (SLAs).** This is achieved by establishing a **structured and well-defined process** that governs the entire **incident lifecycle**, from detection to resolution.

Key Objectives of the Incident Management Process:

1. **Timely Resolution**

   To define and follow a clear, time-bound approach that ensures every incident is managed within defined SLA timelines, promoting accountability and service reliability

2. **Ownership and Accountability**

   To record every incident and assign clear ownership, ensuring that each incident is tracked, managed, and resolved with full responsibility from start to finish

3. **Seamless Integration with Other ITSM Processes**

   To maintain consistent collaboration with other IT Service Management processes such as:

   - **Configuration Management** (ensuring the CMDB is updated with incident-related data),
   - **Problem Management** (for root cause analysis), and
   - **Change Management** (when incidents require changes to be made for resolution or prevention).

4. **Data Integrity and Knowledge Sharing**

   To ensure that the Known Error Database (KEDB) and Configuration Management Database (CMDB) are consistently updated with incident-related insights for future reference and proactive risk mitigation

Relationship with Problem and Change Management

An effective Incident Management process often acts as the **trigger point** for initiating both **Problem Management** and **Change Management,** depending on the nature and recurrence of the issue:

- Problem Management is initiated when an incident suggests deeper, underlying issues that require root cause investigation and long-term fixes
- Change Management may be invoked when the resolution of an incident involves configuration changes, system updates, or infrastructure modifications.

Each of these processes is governed under the **ITIL (Information Technology Infrastructure Library)** framework, which offers standardized best practices to manage service delivery, risk, and continuous improvement.

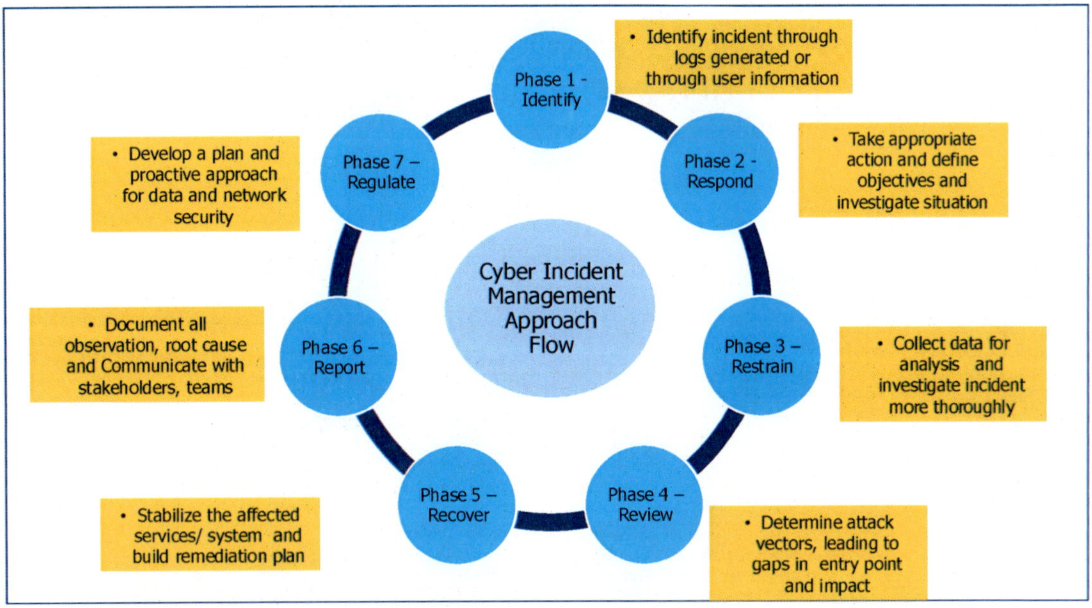

Figure 49 Incident Management Process Workflow for representation

3. CCMP Playbook

Cyber Crisis Incident Management is fundamentally a **reactive strategy** - it kicks in **after** a threat or breach has occurred. While reactive measures like **Incident, Problem, and Change Management** policies are essential to maintain control during chaos, they alone are **not enough** to manage modern, complex cyber threats effectively.

What truly empowers an organization during a cyber crisis is **proactive preparedness** - this is where the **Cyber Crisis Management Playbook (CCMP)** and **Incident Response (IR) Playbooks** come into play.

From Reaction to Readiness: The Role of Playbooks

An **Incident Response Playbook** is a pre-defined, step-by-step guide that outlines how to respond to specific types of cyber incidents - whether it's a ransomware attack, data breach, insider threat, or DDoS incident. It defines roles, responsibilities, communication workflows, escalation paths, and containment steps to be taken **under pressure.**

- A guide book that provides detailed procedures and steps to proactively plan, detect, respond, mitigate, and recover from incidents.
- The runbook / playbook document enables to identify and define roles and responsibilities of all related key stakeholders and business owners along with processes, policies & prevention plans to defend your organization.
- The playbook enables developing a Cyber drill simulation scenario to reactive to such incident
- To gauge an organizations level of readiness to counter threat

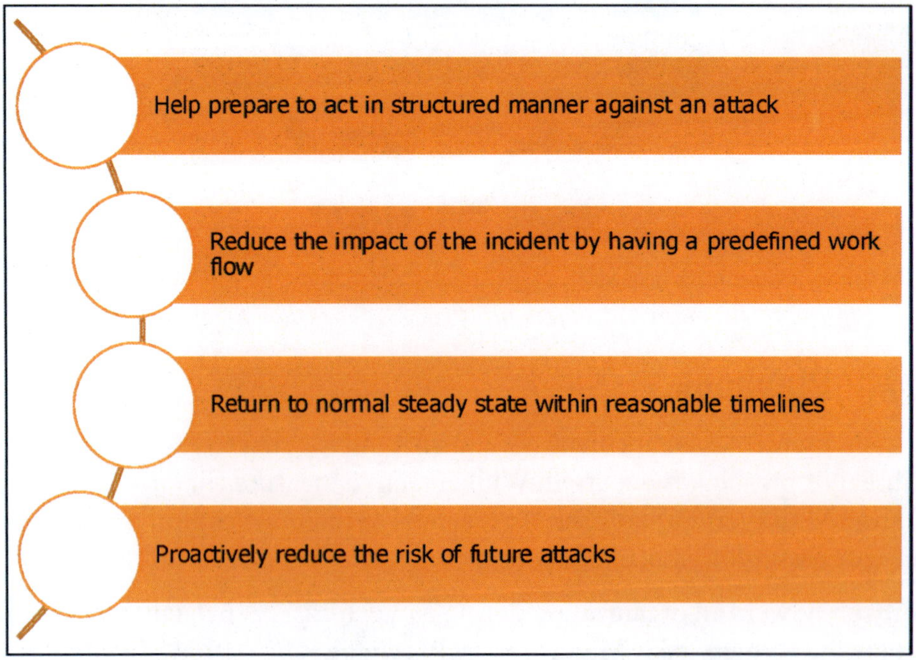

Figure 50 Incident Response Playbook Objective

Structured Incident Response Framework: A Phased Approach

An effective **Incident Response (IR) Framework** is not built ad hoc - it must be structured, strategic, and based on industry-accepted standards. One of the most widely recognized and practical guides for establishing a robust incident response capability is the **NIST Special Publication 800-61 Revision 2** - Computer Security Incident Handling Guide.

This NIST framework outlines a **phased, lifecycle-based approach** to incident response, ensuring organizations can handle incidents systematically and minimize impact.

NIST-Based Four-Phase Incident Response Lifecycle:

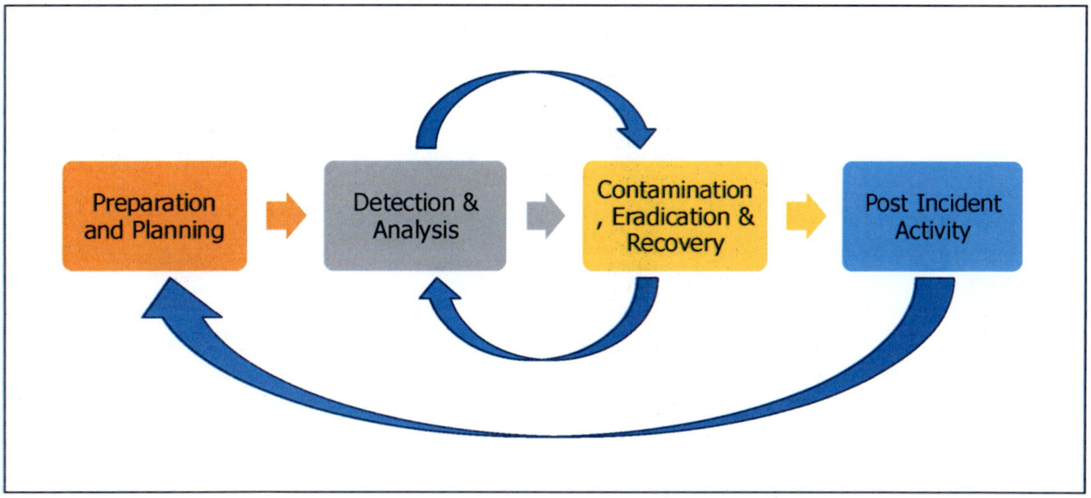

Figure 51 NIST Approach towards Computer Security Incident Handling

1. **Preparation**
    - o Establish policies, response teams, communication plans, and tools
    - o Conduct training and simulations (cyber drills, tabletop exercises)
    - o Ensure logging, alerting, and backups are in place
2. **Detection and Analysis**
    - o Identify signs of an incident (e.g., unusual traffic, alerts, system anomalies)
    - o Analyze data from SIEM, logs, threat intelligence feeds, and endpoints
    - o Categorize and prioritize the incident based on impact and urgency

3. **Containment, Eradication, and Recovery**
    - o **Containment:** Stop the spread - isolate infected systems or segments
    - o **Eradication:** Remove root cause (e.g., malware, compromised accounts)
    - o **Recovery:** Restore systems and validate their integrity before reintroduction
4. **Post-Incident Activity**
    - o Conduct a lessons-learned review (Post-Incident Review - PIR)
    - o Document findings and update IR playbooks and security controls
    - o Feed insights into vulnerability management and threat hunting

By adopting a NIST-based IR framework, organizations ensure their Cyber Crisis Management Plan (CCMP) aligns with **global best practices,** enhances **response maturity,** and promotes a **continuous improvement cycle** in their security posture.

Before drafting a robust **Incident Response (IR) Plan** or designing specific **IR Playbooks,** it is crucial to understand the foundational elements that influence how an organization prepares and responds to cyber threats.

Each **cyber-attack scenario**-whether it's a **malware infection, ransomware outbreak, DDoS attack, phishing attempt,** or **data theft**-requires **unique response strategies.** Therefore, having **clarity upfront** on the variables that influence response actions is critical to building an effective, tailored response mechanism.

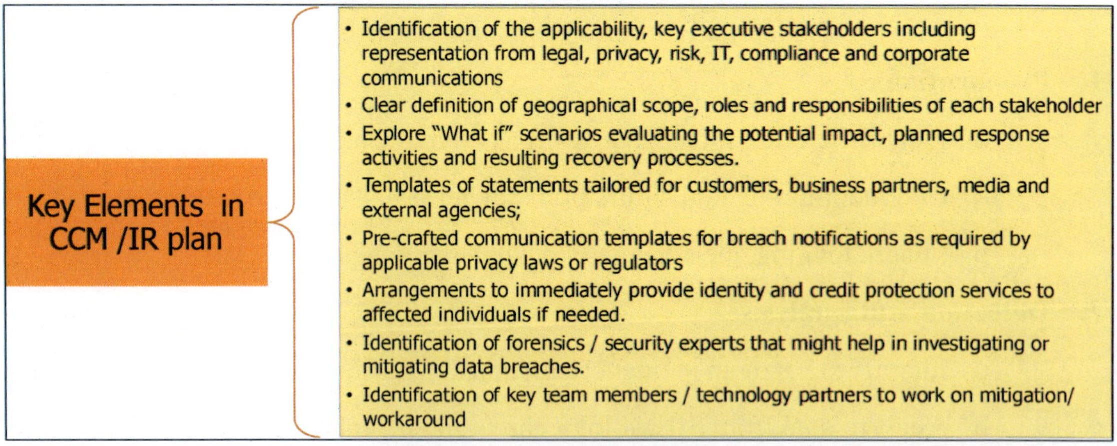

Figure 52 Cyber Crisis Management and Incident Response Plan Considerations

Mapping of the key elements as per above mentioned and aligning it to NIST guidelines is one of the recommended approach which will help to ensure that the IR plans run's horizontal as well vertically across the organization. The following table runs through the activities which can be considered as part of IR plan across 4 phases and 6 tracks:

Preparation

- Review and build an organizational security policy,
- Conduct risk assessment and identify sensitive and critical assets,
- Classify and categorize which are critical security incidents which the team should focus
- Build an Incident Response team and other playbooks

Identification, Detect and Analysis

- Monitor IT systems and its logs
- Triage and do an analysis of the entire events and the workflow
- Detect deviations from normal operations and qualify it for actual security incidents
- Collect more evidence, determine the possible impact establish its type and severity, and document everything

Containment

- Perform short-term containment
- Isolate system or network segment or location as per the impact
- Focus on long-term containment, which involves temporary fixes to allow systems to be used in production, while rebuilding clean systems
- Copy / Image the data as per requirement for doing further forensics

Eradication

- Discuss within to decide and plan to eradicate
- Remove malware from all affected systems, or reformat the system or clean /wipe data as per nature of attack and its impact to IT environment

Recovery

- Bring affected production systems back online carefully, to prevent additional attacks

- Test, verify and monitor affected systems to ensure they are back to normal activity
- Re-review the entire IT and business process flow to check all IT controls as required at entry and exits point are strengthened

Post Incident Activity

- Perform a review and post mortem of the incident
- Identify the root cause of the attack, and take action to prevent similar attacks in the future
- Prepare complete documentation of the incident, investigate the incident further, understand what was done to contain it and whether anything in the incident response process could be improved

A template for a typical ransomware playbook is provided below to aid understanding. It is important to note that scenarios may differ across organizations and must be tailored to specific operational environments and requirements. Since incidents can impact multiple dimensions-including confidentiality, integrity, availability, and privacy-it is essential to assess risks comprehensively. This includes involving stakeholders from compliance, operations, legal, and other relevant functions.

Modern SaaS platforms powered by AI and ML technologies can significantly enhance the effectiveness of cyber drills by automating and augmenting traditional manual approaches.

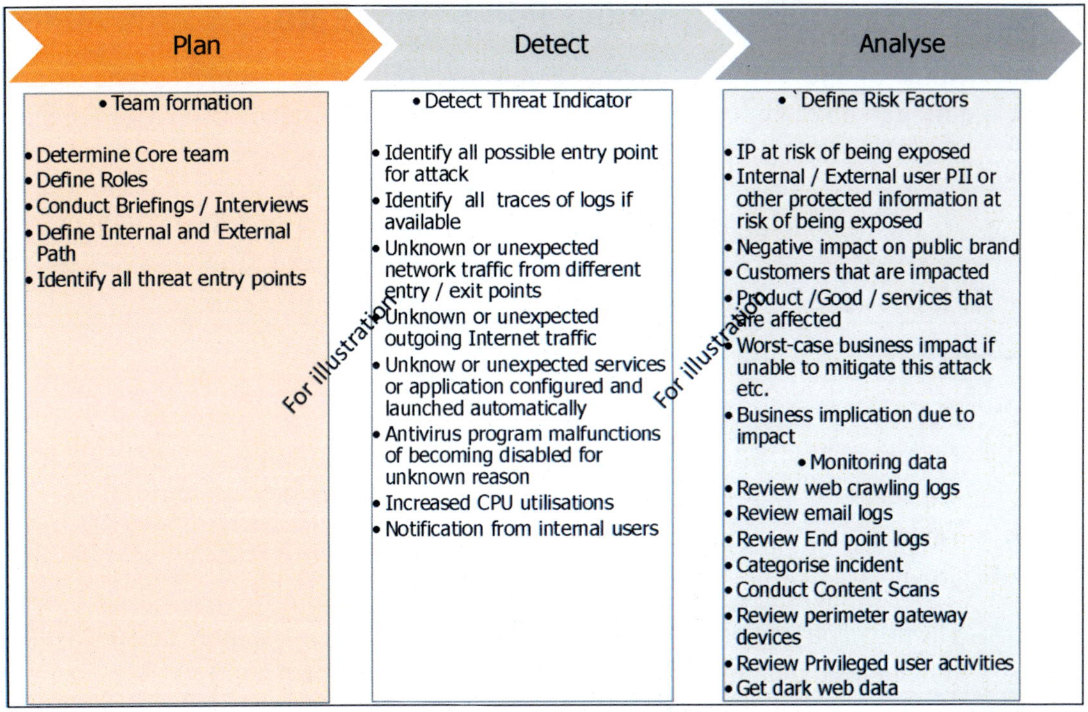

Figure 53 Ransomware Playbook Plan – Detect – Analyse phase for illustration

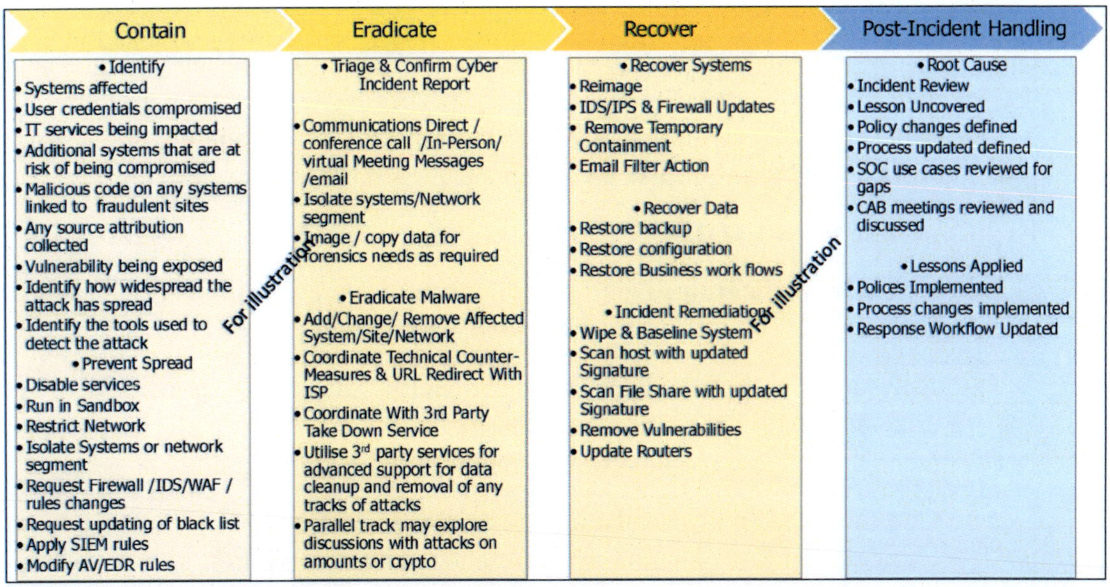

Figure 54 Ransomware Playbook - Contain-Eradicate-Recover-Post Incident Handling Phase

4. Sample Crisis Management Policy Template

A sample template policy presented below for reference only. This is subject to change and may be required to be modified, customised to meet individual needs and requirements.

Objective:

Prepare for and manage large-scale cyber crisis by implementing proactive planning, coordinated response, and continuous improvement measures to mitigate impact and ensure swift recovery.

1. Scope

This policy applies to:

- All critical infrastructure, applications, networks, and data that could be impacted by a cyber crisis
- The organization's leadership, cybersecurity teams, and any personnel involved in crisis response
- The protocols and procedures for responding to cyber crisis, including detection, containment, communication, recovery, and post-incident analysis

2. Policy Statements

2.1 Establish a Cyber Crisis Management Plan (CCMP)

- **Objective:** Develop and maintain a comprehensive Cyber Crisis Management Plan (CCMP) that outlines the steps to be taken during a cyber crisis, from initial detection to post-incident review. The CCMP should include strategies for preventing, mitigating, and recovering from cyber-attacks that disrupt business operations.
- **Key Components of CCMP:**
    - **Crisis Identification:** Define what constitutes a cyber crisis (e.g., large-scale data breach, ransomware attack, critical system compromise)
    - **Roles and Responsibilities:** Assign specific roles and responsibilities to crisis management team members, including the crisis leadership team, technical response team, communications team, and legal team
    - **Communication Protocols:** Establish internal and external communication channels for disseminating accurate and timely information to employees, customers, stakeholders, and regulatory bodies

- **Impact Analysis:** Identify and categorize critical assets and processes that need protection during a crisis.
- **Define** Recovery Time Objectives (RTO) and Recovery Point Objectives (RPO) to prioritize recovery efforts
- **Resource Allocation:** Allocate necessary resources, including personnel, tools, and financial support, to effectively handle a cyber crisis

2.2 Form a Cyber Crisis Response Team (CCRT)

- **Team Composition:** Establish a Cyber Crisis Response Team (CCRT) consisting of key individuals across various departments, including cybersecurity, IT, legal, communications, operations, and senior management
- **Responsibilities:**
  - **Crisis Leadership:** Senior management, including the Chief Information Security Officer (CISO) and the CEO, should lead the crisis response efforts, ensuring alignment with overall business objectives
  - **Technical Experts:** IT and security teams should take the lead in containing the cyber threat, neutralizing the attack, and restoring systems
  - **Communications and Stakeholder Management:** The communications team should be responsible for managing internal and external communication, ensuring transparency and mitigating reputational risks
  - **Legal and Compliance:** Legal teams should ensure compliance with regulatory requirements, handle legal reporting, and assess the potential liabilities arising from the cyber crisis
  - **Team Training:** Ensure that all members of the CCRT are trained regularly on crisis response protocols, decision-making under pressure, and communication strategies

2.3 Conduct Simulations and Tabletop Exercises

- **Objective:** Regularly test and refine the crisis response plan through realistic simulations and tabletop exercises to ensure the team is prepared for various cyber crisis scenarios.

- **Simulation Scenarios:**
    - **Ransomware Attack:** Simulate a ransomware attack affecting critical business operations, requiring immediate containment, communication, and recovery
    - **Data Breach:** Simulate a data breach involving customer or employee data, including notification procedures and regulatory reporting
    - **Denial-of-Service (DoS) Attack:** Simulate a large-scale Distributed Denial-of-Service (DDoS) attack that disrupts online services and business operations
    - **Insider Threat:** Simulate an insider threat scenario where a trusted employee or contractor intentionally or unintentionally compromises systems
- **Tabletop Exercise:** Organize tabletop exercises where the CCRT walk through different crisis scenarios, discussing response actions, decisions, and communication flows. These exercises should focus on decision-making, coordination, and process improvement.
- **Post-Exercise Evaluation:** After each simulation or tabletop exercise, conduct a debriefing session to review the actions taken, lessons learned, and areas for improvement. Use these insights to update and improve the Cyber Crisis Management Plan (CCMP) and the overall crisis response capability.
- **Develop and Implement a Crisis Communication Strategy**
- **Internal Communication:** Define the channels and methods for communicating with internal stakeholders during a cyber crisis. This includes senior management, affected departments, and employees. Ensure transparency while protecting sensitive information.
- **External Communication:** Develop a strategy for communicating with external stakeholders, including customers, regulatory bodies, media, and vendors. Ensure that external communication aligns with the legal requirements, minimizes reputational damage, and provides clarity on the organization's response efforts.
- **Crisis Communication Templates:** Prepare pre-drafted communication templates for various types of cyber crisis. These templates should be customizable to reflect the specifics of the incident but provide a starting point for rapid communication.

2.4 Cyber Crisis Recovery and Post-Incident Analysis

- **Recovery Strategies:** Following containment, implement recovery strategies as outlined in the CCMP, restoring systems, applications, and services based on their criticality and recovery priorities.
- **Root Cause Analysis:** Conduct a thorough root cause analysis (RCA) to identify the vulnerabilities and weaknesses that led to the cyber crisis. This analysis should inform future security strategies and process improvements.
- **Post-Incident Reporting:** Prepare a detailed incident report documenting the crisis response timeline, the impact of the crisis, lessons learned, and recommendations for enhancing cybersecurity measures.
- **Continuous Improvement:** Use lessons learned from each crisis and tabletop exercise to update and refine the CCMP, ensuring it evolves based on new threats, business changes, and improvements in incident response practices.

2.5 Roles and Responsibilities

- **Crisis Management Team (CMT)**
  - Oversee the development and execution of the Cyber Crisis Management Plan
  - Ensure that all team members are trained and equipped to handle cyber crisis effectively
  - Communicate with internal and external stakeholders during a crisis.
- **Cyber Crisis Response Team (CCRT)**
  - Execute the Cyber Crisis Management Plan during a crisis
  - Take immediate action to contain and mitigate the impact of a cyber incident
  - Manage recovery and restore operations in alignment with business continuity objectives
- **IT and Security Teams**
  - Lead the technical response during a crisis, including containing and neutralizing threats, performing forensic analysis, and restoring systems
  - Ensure secure communications and data protection during recovery efforts

- **Communications and PR Teams**
  - Manage internal and external communications during and after a cyber crisis
  - Ensure that messaging is clear, accurate, and aligned with the organization's reputation management goals
- **Legal and Compliance Teams**
  - Ensure legal compliance and regulatory reporting requirements are met.
  - Manage legal liabilities and assist in handling litigation and breach notifications.

By adopting this policy and implementing these practices, the organization ensures it is prepared to manage cyber crisis effectively, minimizing potential damage, maintaining business continuity, and continuously improving its cybersecurity posture.

5. Conclusion

The Cyber Crisis Management Plan (CCMP) serves as a vital framework for effectively countering cyberattacks and cyber terrorism. Conducting cyber drill simulations plays a key role in ensuring that organizations are well-prepared to respond to various attack scenarios. As part of regulatory compliance, regular cyber drills are often mandatory, reinforcing the need for CCMP and IT incident response plans to be dynamic, actively maintained programs within the organization. Successful implementation requires the engagement and coordination of all relevant stakeholders, including management.

This section highlights the critical importance of integrating the CCMP into the broader Governance, Risk, and Compliance (GRC) program, positioning it as an essential, near-mandatory requirement for organizations of all sizes.

Chapter

12

GRC in IT Infrastructure Library (ITIL)

1. Introduction

Governance, Risk Management, and Compliance (GRC) is a holistic approach that integrates an organization's overall governance, enterprise risk management, and adherence to regulatory requirements. A well-designed GRC framework provides a structured methodology to strengthen the Information Security Management System (ISMS) by leveraging a combination of guidelines, standards, and best practices.

The IT Infrastructure Library (ITIL) framework offers a comprehensive set of best practices focused on the delivery and management of IT services. ITIL's primary goal is to standardize IT service management (ITSM) to effectively support business objectives.

GRC can be viewed as a broader approach that complements ITIL by addressing critical areas of service delivery, strategy, and operations at a granular level. In large enterprises, GRC and ITIL often run as parallel streams with significant overlap. While ITIL primarily emphasizes service performance, service level agreements (SLAs), and operational efficiency, GRC extends this scope by incorporating core principles such as confidentiality, integrity, and availability (CIA) alongside regulatory compliance and risk management.

The following figures illustrate how GRC and ITIL frameworks align and work together to enhance organizational resilience and service

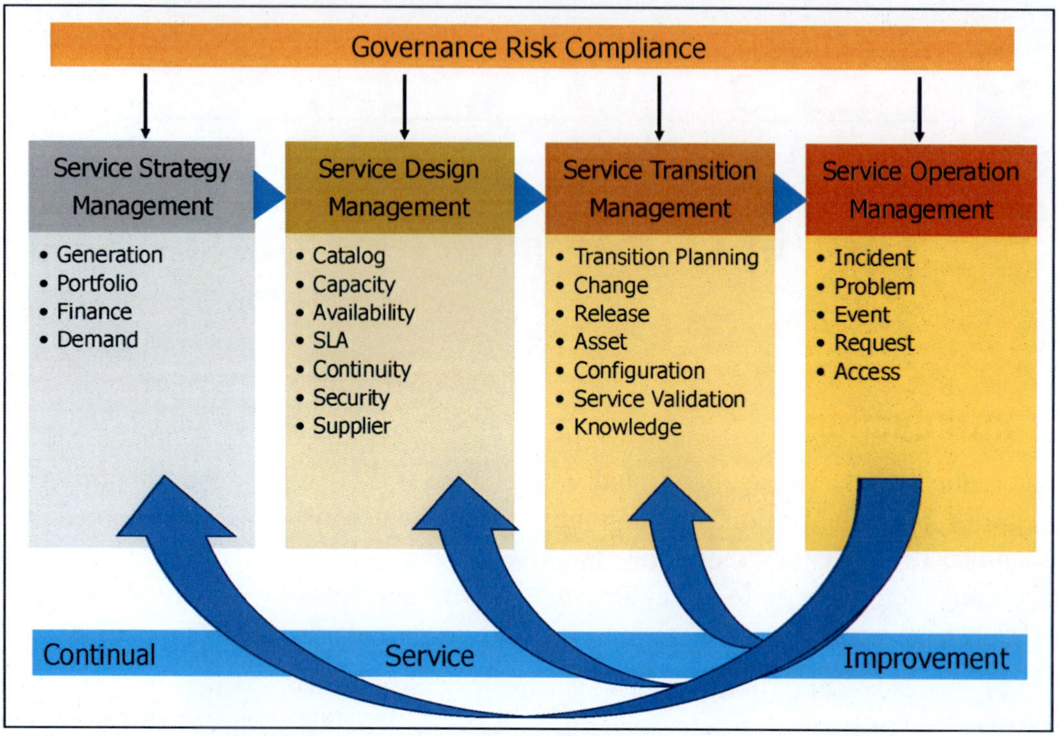

Figure 55 Integrated ITIL and GRC

1. **GRC** works at the apex level broadly defining the overall structure more from risk management perspective in relations to business requirements and aligning to regulations and standards
2. **Service Strategy** which is first layer of ITIL life cycle, determines what capabilities will need to be developed or implemented, including the definition of markets, the development of assets or the necessary preparations for deployment.
3. **Service Design** is the second stage in ITIL where services are defined , sized and foundation laid for build and subsequent transition
4. **Service Transition** is the third stage of the ITIL life cycle which has all elements required to move the services in production mode
5. **Service Operation** is the fourth stage is considering the ongoing task's requirement to run the services and delivery as per defined in design phase
6. **Continual Service Improvement** addresses the requirements related to upgrades, updates and enhancement of operations, so as to align with set strategies and objectives

2. GRC Audit and ITIL layers

As part of any GRC audit or assessment—whether focusing on IT General Controls (ITGC), ISO 27001 standards, regulatory compliance, or other frameworks-each has a defined structure that can be mapped alongside the ITIL layers.

This alignment enables a clear understanding of how governance, risk management, and compliance requirements integrate with IT service management processes, ensuring comprehensive coverage across the entire service lifecycle. The table maps the GRC with ITIL at high level.

GRC	ITIL
• Policy documents which define organisation context, roles responsibilities, scope coverage or statement of applicability with boundaries conditions.	Service Strategy considering Portfolio,
• Framework defining the different IT domains which are to be covered	Service Design, Transition, Operations
• Control objective and controls requirement defining what is to be considered with in each domain	Transition, Operations

Each area within the ITIL framework has a distinct focus and addresses specific functions independently. These areas are governed by their own policy documents, supported by operational procedures and relevant technology controls. To ensure the effective functioning of IT business processes, the core principles of Confidentiality, Integrity, and Availability (C-I-A) of Information System Security apply across all these areas.

The table below presents a high-level overview of the focus and scope for each ITIL area:

1. **Event and Incident Management :** Focus on how to quickly identify, analyse, respond and recover from any incident leading to a system outage / down time of business process
2. **Change Management :** Focus on how to approach towards implementing any changes within the IT infrastructure, after taking concurrence and approval from all stake holders, while ensuring minimal disruption in services after considering all risks and also a plan for rollback in, case changes are not done successfully

3. **Problem Management**: Focus on eliminating the root cause of recurring incidents and reducing the likely hood
4. **Service Level Management:** For different types of incidents (critical , medium , low) what is expected response and recovery time which is to be monitored and managed, and applicable to all internal and external service providers and OEM
5. **Asset Management:** Focus on effective monitoring , management and control of the entire asset usage life cycle with the business operations right from procurement, deployment and disposal
6. **Patch and Release Management:** Both focus on updates and upgrades to IT assets / application / operating system for either fixing the bugs or enhancing the performance or addition of features
7. **Configuration Management :** IT systems / devices / OS when deployed out the box are open and have all services , ports and protocols deployed as per default configuration, which leaves the system vulnerable. Configuration management process helps to hardening the system parameters thereby reducing threats
8. **Capacity Management :** Focus on monitoring the performance of the system to which it is designed and based on the needs define the changes in the capacity in areas of CPU speed, memory , disk storage and other system resources
9. **Access Management :** Focus of providing controlled access to required system resources on need-to-know need-to-do basis
10. **Business Continuity :** In case of any down time or service outage how is the continuity of operations to be defined considering people, process and technology

3. Sample Change Management Process - Policy

The change management sample policy is presented for reference only . This may need to be customized and modified to meet the individual requirements and needs. The roles are responsibilities are indicative and subject to change based on organisational structure.

Objective:

Minimize risks to the organization's IT environment by ensuring that all changes to systems, applications, and infrastructure are thoroughly evaluated, tested, approved, and documented.

1. Scope

This policy applies to all:

- **Changes:** Planned, emergency, and routine changes to hardware, software, network configurations, and application environments
- **Stakeholders**: IT teams, business units, system owners, and external vendors involved in change implementation
- **Assets:** IT systems, applications, and infrastructure components

2. Policy Statements

a. Change Management Policy and Approval Workflow

- Establish a Change Management Policy that outlines the process for evaluating, approving, and implementing changes
    - Categorize changes as standard, normal, or emergency with defined workflows for each category
    - Require formal change requests to include:
        - Description of the change
        - Business justification
        - Estimated impact and risks
        - Testing and implementation plans
    - Ensure all change requests are reviewed and approved by the Change Advisory Board (CAB) or designated approvers based on criticality

b. Risk Assessment and Testing

- Conduct a Risk Assessment for all changes to identify potential impacts, including:
    - Service disruptions
    - Security vulnerabilities
    - Compliance risks
- Mandate thorough testing of changes in a non-production environment before deployment

  - o Include functional, integration, and security testing
  - o Document test results and approvals before moving to production

c. Change Documentation and Logging

- Maintain a change log to record details of all changes, including:
  - o Change request ID
  - o Requestor and approver details
  - o Date and time of implementation
  - o Systems and assets affected
- Include rollback plans in all change requests to ensure rapid recovery in case of failures.

d. Emergency Changes

- Define a streamlined process for emergency changes to address critical issues requiring immediate attention
  - o Obtain expedited approvals with post-implementation review by the CAB.
  - o Document the incident, justification, and actions taken.

e. Post-Implementation Review (PIR)

- Conduct a post-implementation review for significant changes to:
  - o Assess whether objectives were achieved.
  - o Identify issues encountered during implementation.
  - o Update processes based on lessons learned.
- Periodically review change logs, risk assessments, and approval workflows for compliance with the policy.

3. Roles and Responsibilities

▪ **Change Requestor**

- Submit detailed change requests and provide required documentation

- **Change Advisory Board (CAB)**
  - Review and approve or reject change requests based on risk, impact, and alignment with business objectives
  - Include representatives from IT, business units, and security teams
- **IT Operations Team**
  - Implement approved changes as per defined plans
  - Monitor systems post-implementation to identify any adverse effects
- **CISO**
  - Ensure security risks associated with changes are adequately addressed
  - Oversee emergency change processes for compliance
- **Internal Audit Team**
  - Review of the documentation of the change management process and procedures
  - Review adherance and compliance wrt to policies and adopted standards

4. Change Management Checklist

The change management checklist is presented to help understand the different activities to be considered as part of pre and post change implement . This is generic checklist and may need to be customized and modified to meet the individual requirements and needs. The checklist apart from activities should clearly have the ownership defined and identified so that it runs smoothly. Based on the type of changes , i.e. standard change, critical change, emergency change certain steps can be merged or at times with approvals can be bypassed after seeking necessary proposal approvals from management

	Change Management Checklist		
Step	**Task**	**Owner**	**Status (✓/✗)**
1	Identify and document the change request	Requestor	
2	Define change type (Standard/Normal/Emergency)	Change Manager	
3	Conduct Vulnerability & Patch Assessment (Review CVEs, vendor advisories, CERT-In alerts)	Security Team	
4	Classify vulnerabilities (Critical/High/Medium/Low) and define remediation timeline	Security Team	
5	Conduct Impact Assessment (CIA Triad: Confidentiality, Integrity, Availability)	Change Manager	
6	Obtain approvals from Business, IT, and Security Teams	CAB	
7	Schedule patching and change implementation	IT Operations	
8	Conduct testing in a staging environment	IT Operations	
9	Deploy patches and changes in the production environment	IT Operations	
10	Perform post-implementation testing and verification	IT Operations	
11	Update asset inventory, patch logs, and security documentation	IT & Security Teams	
12	Conduct post-change review with stakeholders	Change Manager	

	Post-Change Implementation Checklist		
Step	**Task**	**Owner**	**Status (✓/✗)**
1	Verify change was successfully implemented	IT Team	
2	Conduct post-change testing to ensure stability	IT Team	
3	Monitor system logs for anomalies	IT Security	
4	Update change management system with implementation details	Change Manager	
5	Document lessons learned, including issues faced and solutions	IT Team	
6	Update asset inventory and patch management logs	IT Security	
7	Notify stakeholders about change completion	Change Manager	
8	Validate compliance requirements (SEBI CSCRF, CERT-In, etc.)	Compliance Team	
9	Conduct post-implementation review with CAB	Change Manager	
10	Officially close change request and archive documentation	Change Manager	

Figure 56 Change Management Checklist for Illustration

5. Sample Incident Management and Response Policy

The incident management sample policy is presented for reference only . This may need to be customized and modified to meet the individual requirements and needs. The roles are responsibilities are indicative and subject to change based on organisational structure.

Objective:

Establish robust processes to detect, report, respond to, and mitigate cybersecurity incidents efficiently, minimizing their impact on business operations and preventing recurrence.

1. Scope

This policy applies to all:

- Cybersecurity incidents affecting the organization's IT and operational systems, applications, data, and personnel
- Internal and external stakeholders involved in incident reporting, management, and mitigation
- Vendors and third-party service providers engaged with organizational systems

2. Policy Statements

a. Incident Reporting and Escalation Procedures

- Define a standardized incident reporting process to ensure timely detection and communication of incidents.
  - o Establish a 24/7 incident reporting channel, such as a dedicated email, hotline, or ticketing system
  - o Mandate reporting of any suspected or confirmed incidents within one hour of detection
  - o Categorize incidents by severity (e.g., critical, high, medium, low) and assign appropriate escalation paths
- Ensure all incidents are logged with detailed information, including:
  - o Date and time of detection
  - o Systems or assets impacted
  - o Description of the incident
  - o Initial assessment of severity and potential impact

b. Incident Response Plan (IRP)

- Develop and maintain an Incident Response Plan (IRP) to provide a structured approach for managing incidents
  - Clearly define incident response stages: Identification, Containment, Eradication, Recovery, and Lessons Learned
  - Review and update the IRP annually or after major incidents

c. Incident Response Drills

- Conduct regular drills and simulations to test and enhance the effectiveness of the IRP, including:
  - Table top exercises to validate communication protocols and decision-making
  - Technical simulations (e.g., mock ransomware attack) to test containment and recovery measures
- Include third-party vendors in drills if their services are critical to the organization
- Document outcomes and action plans for improvement based on drill findings

d. Documentation and Incident Analysis

- Maintain detailed records of all incidents, including:
  - Root cause analysis (RCA).
  - Steps taken to mitigate the incident.
  - Timeline of response activities.
  - Impact assessment on business operations and stakeholders.
- Analyze incident trends and root causes to identify recurring vulnerabilities and implement preventive controls

3. Roles and Responsibilities

Incident Manager

- Oversee the incident response process and coordinate cross-functional teams
- Ensure timely communication and escalation of critical incidents

Technical Teams

- Perform initial analysis, containment, and recovery of impacted systems

- Collaborate with security vendors or partners, if required, to resolve incidents

CISO

- Approve the IRP and oversee its execution during incidents
- Ensure regulatory reporting requirements for significant incidents are met

Employees

- Immediately report suspected or observed security incidents
- Comply with instructions during incident response to minimize impact

Internal Audit Team

- Review incident documentation and provide feedback for process improvement
- Verify compliance with incident management procedures during audits

6. Incident Management Procedure Template

The template is for reference only. Many regulatory bodies have a defined format which is mandated to be used to reporting different types of incidents.

Sr.No	
Date and Time Incident Occurred	
Physical location of the Incident	
Type of incident	
Systems / Information Affected	
No of Host Affected	
Summary of the incident	
The current state of Incident	
List of evidence gathered	
Actions taken by incident handlers	
Root cause analysis	
Next step to be taken	

Figure 57 Incident Management and Response Template for illustration

7. Conclusion

The ITIL framework not only addresses IT General Controls (ITGC), but also reinforces the Confidentiality, Integrity, and Availability of enterprise data-ensuring that IT operations align with defined policies and processes. Key areas such as service delivery, service operations, and continuous improvement are critical to maintaining the seamless, efficient, and optimized performance of all digital business functions.

By ensuring these areas perform as intended, organizations inherently strengthen their operational governance and risk management. Together, the GRC and ITIL frameworks complement each other, enabling organizations to uphold robust Information System Security while consistently delivering service excellence.

Chapter

13

Artificial Intelligence Associated Risk and GRC

1. Introduction

The growing adoption of Artificial Intelligence (AI) is reshaping industries by enabling higher levels of automation, smarter decision-making, and deeper insights through advanced data analysis. Across sectors, organizations are increasingly leveraging AI-powered solutions to optimize operations, enhance customer experiences, and drive innovation.

However, as AI technologies become more pervasive, they bring with them a unique set of risks and challenges. These include concerns related to data privacy, algorithmic bias, transparency, accountability, and potential misuse. The rapid pace of AI development also often outstrips regulatory frameworks, creating gaps in compliance and governance that organizations must proactively address. Consequently, there is an urgent need for robust Governance, Risk Management, and Compliance (GRC) frameworks tailored to AI to ensure responsible, ethical, and safe deployment of these technologies.

2. AI basics

Artificial Intelligence, in its simplest form, refers to systems that can learn from data inputs to make decisions, predictions, or generate outputs that impact real-world processes. These systems rely on machine learning models that identify patterns in historical data and apply this knowledge to new, unseen data.

Traditional AI typically focuses on performing a defined task intelligently within specific parameters. For example, fraud detection systems, recommendation engines, or voice recognition tools operate based on algorithms and training data that guide their behavior. While these systems can adapt and improve over time by learning from new data, their decision-making remains confined to predefined rules and environments. They excel in optimizing routine and well-structured problems, but do not possess creativity or the ability to generate entirely new content or concepts.

In contrast, **Generative AI** marks a significant leap forward. These systems do not just respond to inputs, but actively create new content-such as natural language text, images, music, or even software code - by learning complex underlying data patterns. Gen AI Models demonstrate this capability by generating outputs that can mimic human creativity and innovation. However, this transformative ability also introduces new risks, such as generating misleading or harmful content, deepfakes, intellectual property concerns, and ethical dilemmas around authorship and originality.

- AI systems enable machines to perceive their environment and uses learning and intelligence to take actions that maximize their chances of achieving defined goals

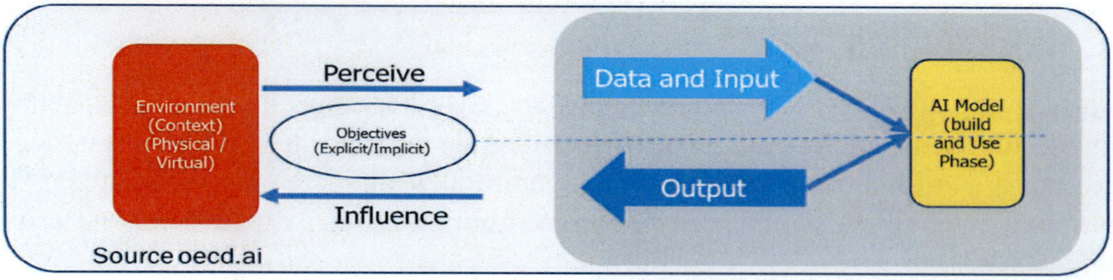

Figure 58 AI System Model

- AI system enables to proactive provide information and predict possible out comes
- AI systems are capable of adapting their behavior to a certain degree by analyzing the effects of previous actions and working autonomously.

3. Risk to AI Model compared to traditional software

While traditional software systems benefit from a mature ecosystem of standards, frameworks, and best practices designed to identify and mitigate associated risks, AI models introduce a distinct and evolving set of challenges.

Unlike conventional software, which follows explicitly programmed logic, AI systems often operate through complex, data-driven learning processes. This leads to risks that are less predictable and harder to detect-such as model bias, lack of explainability, adversarial manipulation, and data drift. As a result, the risk landscape for AI demands new approaches to governance, assurance, and accountability that go beyond traditional software risk management.

- AI systems, for example, may be trained on data that may have changed over time, this may sometimes significantly and unexpectedly, affect system functionality and trustworthiness in ways which may be are hard to understand

- The data used for building an AI system may not be a true, or appropriate representation of the context, or intended use of the AI system, and the ground truth may either not exist or not be available (practical vs predictive)
- Datasets used to train AI systems may become stale or outdated relative to deployment context
- Use of pre-trained models cause issues with bias management, scientific validity, and reproducibility of AI systems
- The contexts in which AI systems are deployed are frequently complex, making it difficult to detect and respond to failures when they occur
- AI systems are inherently socio-technical in nature, meaning they are influenced by societal dynamics and human behavior
- Intentional or unintentional changes during training may fundamentally alter AI system performance
- Higher degree of difficulty in predicting failure modes

4. AI Usage and Cyber Security Managing Challenges

Traditional methods and tools for monitoring and managing the three pillars - confidentiality, availability, and integrity - are no longer proving to be effective to identify, detect and prevent an attack.Threat actors are being far more proactive to quickly identify open loopholes due to constant data gathering from dark and deep web.

Absence of local skilled professionals, having near expertise of ethical hacker or threat actors is further adding to the trouble of near Realtime monitoring and management and providing timely response. All the above is thus hindering the security teams ability to safe guard data, manage access, timely identify threat and respond timely.

Apart from this there is push from business owners to use other AI technologies, which is further adding to the challenges for CISO/CTO. Along with its adoption, there are growing concerns in some areas such as:

- AI enabled social engineering and malware attacks, (targeted attacks by embedding malware in AI codes due to potential of code generation and automation)
- Potential mass volume attacks, autonomous attacks due to its sheer nature of generative features (like DDoS)
- Intrusion attacks with increased speed scale and sophistication

- Many medium skills threat actors who probably did not have the knowledge or the sophistication required early, can make use of the available paid AI for advisories services and launch adversarial attacks
- Lower entry skills leading to increase in the population of threat actors. More attacks, faster attacks and less time to respond for defenders
- Hackers and threat actors resulting in impersonation of users (due to its generative features and usage of data, voice, text, images)
- AI models are doing data analysis by collecting all available types and done by both good and bad users

Some of the content is from IBM Site

5. AI Risks and Governance Challenges

AI systems are not subject to the same controls as traditional code development and there is difficulty in performing regular AI-based software testing, or determining what to test.

AI system may require more ongoing and frequent maintenance and triggers for conducting corrective maintenance due to change in data, model, or concept drift.

Underdeveloped software testing standards and inability to document AI-based practices to the standard is another challenge for conducting AI testing in a uniform manner. There is also Privacy risk due to enhanced data aggregation capability for AI systems.

These risks make AI a uniquely challenging technology to deploy and utilize both for organizations and within society. Without proper controls, AI systems can amplify and provide undesirable outcomes for individuals and communities.

The expanded capabilities of AI, particularly generative models, heighten the need for vigilant risk management and governance. Typical key risks with AI usage include:

- **Bias and Fairness:** AI systems can inadvertently perpetuate or amplify biases present in their training data, leading to unfair or discriminatory outcomes.
- **Transparency and Explainability:** Complex AI models, especially deep learning networks, often function as "black boxes," making it difficult to explain how decisions are made, which complicates accountability.
- **Data Privacy:** AI's reliance on large datasets raises concerns about the collection, use, and protection of sensitive personal information.

- **Security Threats:** AI can both enhance cybersecurity and introduce new vulnerabilities, including adversarial attacks that manipulate AI behavior.
- **Regulatory Compliance:** Emerging laws and standards demand organizations to demonstrate responsible AI use, posing challenges in aligning AI development with evolving requirements.

AI technologies, while transformative, also introduce a wide spectrum of risks that can adversely affect individuals, organizations, communities, society at large, and even the environment and planet. These risks may manifest in various forms-ranging from short-term operational disruptions to long-term systemic consequences. They can be high or low probability events, localized in scope or global in scale, and vary in impact from minimal to highly consequential.

Unlike traditional technologies, AI systems have the potential to autonomously learn, adapt, and influence outcomes in ways that are not always transparent or predictable. This amplifies the complexity and urgency of identifying, assessing, and mitigating associated risks.

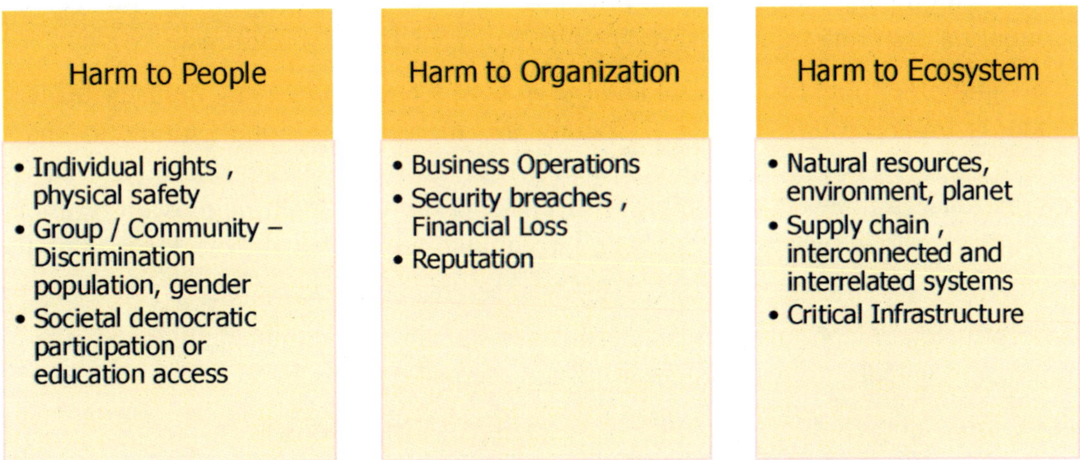

Figure 59 AI Associated Impact-Harms source NIST

Effective AI Risk Management is therefore essential to ensure the responsible design, deployment, and oversight of AI systems. It plays a critical role in safeguarding ethical standards, maintaining public trust, ensuring compliance with regulatory frameworks, and minimizing unintended harm. A robust Risk Management approach helps balance innovation with accountability-allowing AI to deliver benefits while minimizing its potential negative impacts.

6. Role of GRC in AI Management

Integrating AI Risk Management within an organization's broader GRC framework is essential to effectively mitigate these challenges. A strong AI governance program includes establishing policies and controls that address ethical use, data quality, risk assessment, continuous monitoring, and compliance with applicable laws and standards. It also involves stakeholder engagement across legal, IT, compliance, and business units to ensure that AI-driven initiatives align with organizational values and risk appetite.

By embedding GRC principles into AI lifecycle management-from design and development to deployment and ongoing operations-organizations can not only harness AI's potential, but also safeguard against unintended consequences, reputational damage, and regulatory penalties.

With the implementation of proper controls, AI systems can be guided to reduce inequitable outcomes and promote fairness. **Responsible AI practices** ensure that decisions regarding the design, development, and deployment of AI technologies are aligned with human values, ethical principles, and societal goals. These practices are essential for fostering transparency, accountability, inclusivity, and trust.

In recognition of both the promise and the risks of AI, policymakers, industry leaders, standards organizations, and civil society are increasingly collaborating to shape AI in a way that advances economic prosperity while minimizing harm. One of the key reference frameworks in this global effort is the OECD Principles on Artificial Intelligence, which serve as a widely endorsed international benchmark for guiding the responsible development and governance of AI.

These principles emphasize inclusive growth, sustainable development, human-centered values, transparency, robustness, security, and accountability.

Key Global Stakeholders Leading Responsible AI Initiatives:

- EU AI Act: has been released in 2023
- US AI policy in being framed and likely to be released shortly
- Similarly other regional(China, Singapore, Japan, Korea Canada) AI directive are also in pipeline
- NIST AI Risk Management Framework
- ISO42001: 2023 Artificial Intelligence Management Systems (AIMS)

- The Indian government recognized the importance of ethics in AI. Discussions are underway to develop ethical guidelines for the development and deployment of AI technologies.

There are 2 aspects of when we're talking about **Risk to and Risk of AI.** One is the usage part of it and the second one is the building part of it. Some the common points considered for implementing a Risk Management framework by all regions include:

- Adopting a proportionate, risk-based framework based on risk posed to privacy, non-discrimination, fairness
- Take a sectoral approach that builds on existing regulation and that leverage existing regulatory expertise in specific domains, rather than one-size-fits-all horizontal approaches
- Promote an interoperable approach to AI standards and governance given the cross-border nature of usage and operations
- Consistent with the core principles for AI to include human rights, transparency as defined in OECD
- Recognize the importance of transparency so that people understand when they are using or engaging with AI.
- Build AI related in lines with guidelines such as Cybersecurity, data privacy, Intellectual property protection

Source – OECD

Many jurisdictions are increasingly turning to **regulatory sandboxes** as a proactive tool to foster innovation while ensuring public safety and ethical compliance. These sandboxes enable structured collaboration between the private sector and policymakers, allowing for the real-world testing of AI systems under regulatory supervision. This approach not only accelerates the development of safe and responsible AI technologies, but also helps inform the creation of adaptive rules and standards-especially for **higher-risk AI applications** where closer regulatory scrutiny is essential.

To guide the development and deployment of AI systems in a risk-sensitive manner, several regulatory frameworks, including the **EU AI Act,** have introduced a tiered classification model. This model categorizes AI systems based on their potential impact on individuals and society, ensuring that regulatory requirements are proportionate to the level of risk.

Unacceptable risk - Unacceptable risk AI systems are systems which are considered a threat to people and will be banned. They include:

- Cognitive behavioral manipulation of people or specific vulnerable groups: for example, voice-activated toys that encourage dangerous behavior in children
- Social scoring: classifying people based on behavior, socio-economic status or personal characteristics
- Biometric identification and categorization of people
- Real-time and remote biometric identification systems, such as facial recognition

High risk - AI systems that negatively affect safety or fundamental rights will be considered high risk

1) AI systems that are used in products falling under the EU's product safety legislation. This includes toys, aviation, cars, medical devices and lifts.
2) AI systems falling into specific areas that will have to be registered in an EU database:

- Management and operation of critical infrastructure
- Education and vocational training
- Employment, worker management and access to self-employment
- Access to and enjoyment of essential private services and public services and benefits
- Law enforcement
- Migration, asylum and border control management
- Assistance in legal interpretation and application of the law.

Transparency requirements Generative AI, like ChatGPT, will not be classified as high-risk, but will have to comply with transparency requirements and EU copyright law:

- Disclosing that the content was generated by AI
- Designing the model to prevent it from generating illegal content
- Publishing summaries of copyrighted data used for training

Figure 60 AI Rules for different risk level (Source EU act)

7. Risk Management Framework For AI

AI Risk Management is an essential pillar in the **responsible development, deployment, and oversight** of artificial intelligence systems. A well-structured AI risk management framework encourages organizations-and their internal teams involved in designing, developing, and operating AI-to proactively assess the context of AI usage and consider both intended and unintended consequences. By identifying and mitigating potential harms, organizations can significantly enhance the **trustworthiness** of AI systems and foster **public trust** in their use.

Governments and industry bodies across the globe are taking varied approaches to AI governance. While some jurisdictions are opting for **guidance-based frameworks** that emphasize voluntary adherence to responsible AI practices, others are moving toward **regulatory models,** especially in areas where safety, ethics, and privacy risks are deemed substantial. The growing diversity of approaches reflects a shared recognition of the need for context-sensitive, risk-proportionate governance mechanisms.

A common best practice among leading frameworks is the categorization of AI risk based on its application and context of use, rather than the technology itself. Risk levels-typically classified as **high, medium, or low**-guide the intensity of oversight and compliance measures.

Key AI Risk Categories

- **Ethical Risks:** Bias, discrimination, and lack of transparency in decision-making.
- **Governance Risks:** Gaps in accountability, documentation, and auditability of AI processes.
- **Security Risks:** Model poisoning, data breaches, adversarial attacks, and concept drift.
- **Communication Risks:** Misinformation, manipulation, and lack of explainability to users.

Emerging Guidelines and Standards in AI Risk Management

As of the time of writing, several key standards and guidelines are shaping global conversations on AI risk management:

- **ISO/IEC 42001 – AI Management System Standard:**

  ISO standard designed to help organizations establish, implement, maintain, and continually improve an AI Management System (AIMS). It outlines requirements for risk assessment, stakeholder involvement, and lifecycle governance to promote responsible AI use.

- **NIST AI Risk Management Framework (AI RMF) – United States:**

  Developed by the National Institute of Standards and Technology, this framework provides a voluntary, structured approach to identifying and managing AI risks. It promotes trustworthiness by focusing on characteristics such as fairness, accountability, transparency, and robustness.

- **EU Artificial Intelligence Act – European Union:**

  The first comprehensive legislative proposal regulating AI based on its risk category. It outlines specific obligations for high-risk AI systems and bans systems deemed to pose unacceptable risks to fundamental rights.

These frameworks underscore a growing consensus: **AI Risk Management must be dynamic, context-aware, and embedded throughout the AI lifecycle.** Organizations that adopt robust AI governance practices not only reduce exposure to ethical, legal, and reputational risks, but also gain a competitive edge by building trustworthy, human-centered AI systems.

For the purpose of our discussion, we have considered **NIST AI Risk Management Framework (AI RMF)** as a foundational reference. This framework provides a flexible, structured, and voluntary approach that organizations can use to identify, assess, manage, and monitor risks associated with artificial intelligence systems.

At the heart of the AI RMF is the **Core**, which is composed of **four key functions- GOVERN, MAP, MEASURE,** and **MANAGE**. These functions are designed to be applied across the AI system lifecycle and to align with organizational priorities and risk tolerance

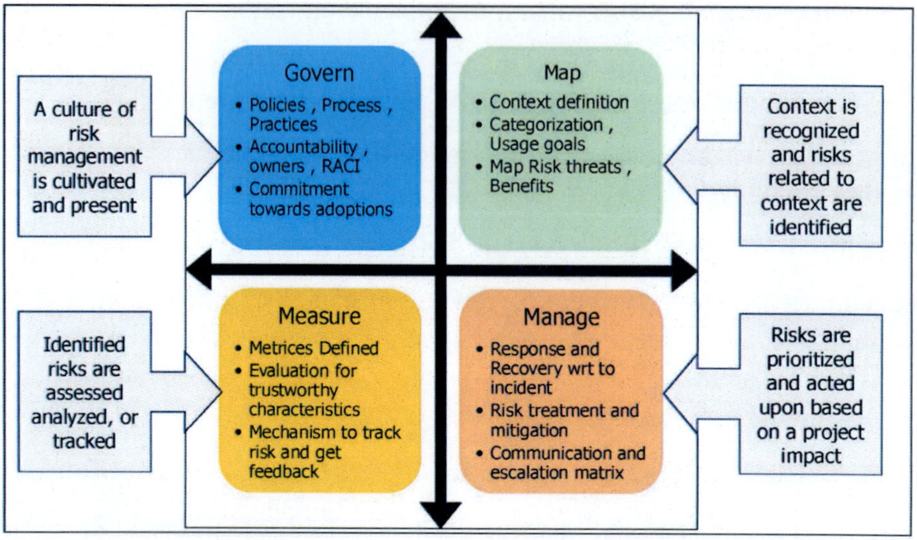

Figure 61 NIST AI RMF (Source NIST)

The GOVERN function:

- Policies, processes, procedures, and practices across the organization related to the mapping, measuring, and managing of AI risks are in place, transparent, and implemented effectively
- Accountability structures are in place so that the appropriate teams and individuals are empowered, responsible, and trained for mapping, measuring, and managing AI risks

<table>
<tr><td>

- Workforce diversity, equity, inclusion, and accessibility processes are prioritized in the mapping, measuring, and managing of AI risks throughout the lifecycle.
- Organizational teams are committed to a culture that considers and communicates AI risk
- Processes are in place for robust engagement with relevant AI actors
- Policies and procedures are in place to address AI risks and benefits arising from third-party software and data and other supply chain issues

</td></tr>
<tr><td>

The MAP Function :

- Context is established and understood
- Categorization of the AI system is performed
- AI capabilities, targeted usage, goals, and expected benefits and costs compared with appropriate benchmarks are understood
- Risks and benefits are mapped for all components of the AI system including third-party software and data
- Impacts to individuals, groups, communities, organizations, and society are characterized

</td></tr>
<tr><td>

The MEASURE function :

- Appropriate methods and metrics are identified and applied
- AI systems are evaluated for trustworthy characteristics
- Mechanisms for tracking identified AI risks over time are in place
- Feedback about efficacy of measurement is gathered and assessed

</td></tr>
<tr><td>

The MANAGE function :

- AI risks based on assessments and other analytical output from the MAP and MEASURE functions are prioritized, responded to, and managed
- Strategies to maximize AI benefits and minimize negative impacts are planned, prepared, implemented, documented, and informed by input from relevant AI actors
- AI risks and benefits from third-party entities are managed
- Risk treatments, including response and recovery, and communication plans for the identified and measured AI risks are documented and monitored regularly

</td></tr>
</table>

8. AI System Audit approach

In alignment with the scope and selected framework-such as ISO/IEC 42001 or the NIST AI Risk Management Framework (AI RMF)-organizations can structure their AI systems to meet the expectations of responsible AI governance. These standards provide foundational guidance for ensuring transparency, fairness, accountability, and security in AI system development and use.

At a high level, the AI system audit and assessment approach can be structured into the following key stages:

Stage	Scope
Audit and Assess	Gap Assessment Audit
	Risk Assessment and AI Impact Assessment
	Awareness Training for Top Management/Stakeholders
Define and Develop	Policy build
	Procedure development
Apply and Implement	Implementation Training
	Policy and procedure implementation oversight
	AIMS alignment documentation with ISO42001/NIST ISMS
Maintain and Manage	Internal Audit Training
	Internal Audit Management Review
	External audit readiness and support

Chapter

14

GRC and Third-Party Risk Management

1. Introduction

In today's interconnected digital landscape, organizations increasingly rely on third-party vendors to deliver a wide array of services within their IT ecosystems. These vendors often have varying levels of access to sensitive systems, applications, and data based on the nature of their engagement.

As regulatory scrutiny around third-party relationships intensifies, it becomes imperative for organizations to build robust capabilities to monitor and manage **vendor risk, compliance, and performance.** Failure to do so can expose organizations to significant operational, reputational, financial, and regulatory risks.

Given that vendors often have access to critical assets and data, it is essential to assess potential operational risks they introduce to IT environments. In addition to ensuring vendor compliance with the organization's internal policies regarding Confidentiality, Integrity, and Availability (CIA), organizations must also ensure adherence to regulatory requirements and regional data protection laws, such as those governing privacy, cybersecurity, and cross-border data transfers.

2. Need for Vendor Risk Management

In the current business environment, third-party vendors are diverse and perform various strategic and operational roles. Depending on the nature of services they provide, and the type of system access required , vendors may fall into one or more of the following categories:

- OEM's of the IT technology stack providers who are supporting the hardware / software assets
- Software developers who are developing business applications on an ongoing basis

- Contract employers or loan staffing professionals working either onsite or remote
- Cloud Service providers who are providing IaaS , PaaS , SaaS services
- Business partners or customers who are working in collaboration with organizations

Considering the compliance, operational, and technology risks arising from the shared use of IT resources with third parties, it is imperative for organizations to establish a robust **Vendor Risk Management Framework** as an integral part of their operational guidelines. This framework enables systematic identification, assessment, and mitigation of risks associated with third-party engagements.

The table below outlines the various types of risks posed by third parties and the potential exposures organizations may face:

Data Leakage and theft	Data Privacy breaches	Regulatory non compliance	Non registered users accessing system
Service Level Agreements	Poor Quality of support	Legal obligation	Cross border rules violation
Data Misuse	Data Duplication	Intellectual Property	Copyright violations

3. Vendor Risk Management Framework Approach

Developing a structured **Vendor Risk Management (VRM) framework** is a critical first step for organizations seeking to effectively manage third-party risks. This framework enables the systematic identification, classification, and oversight of vendors based on the nature and criticality of the business services they provide.

The typical lifecycle of a third-party/vendor engagement includes the following key phases:

- **Profiling and Registration**
- **Onboarding and Risk Assessment**
- **Policy Development and IT Control Implementation**
- **Ongoing Monitoring and Performance Management**
- **Deboarding and Termination**

Each phase requires the involvement of multiple organizational functions to ensure comprehensive risk management. Key stakeholders typically include **Contracts, Legal, Procurement, Human Resources, Administration, IT, Information Security, and Business Unit Owners.**

Similar to an organization-wide ISMS (Information Security Management System), a successful VRM program must be holistic-encompassing **people, processes, and technology**-and be continuously **monitored, measured, and maintained** throughout the entire lifecycle of the vendor relationship.

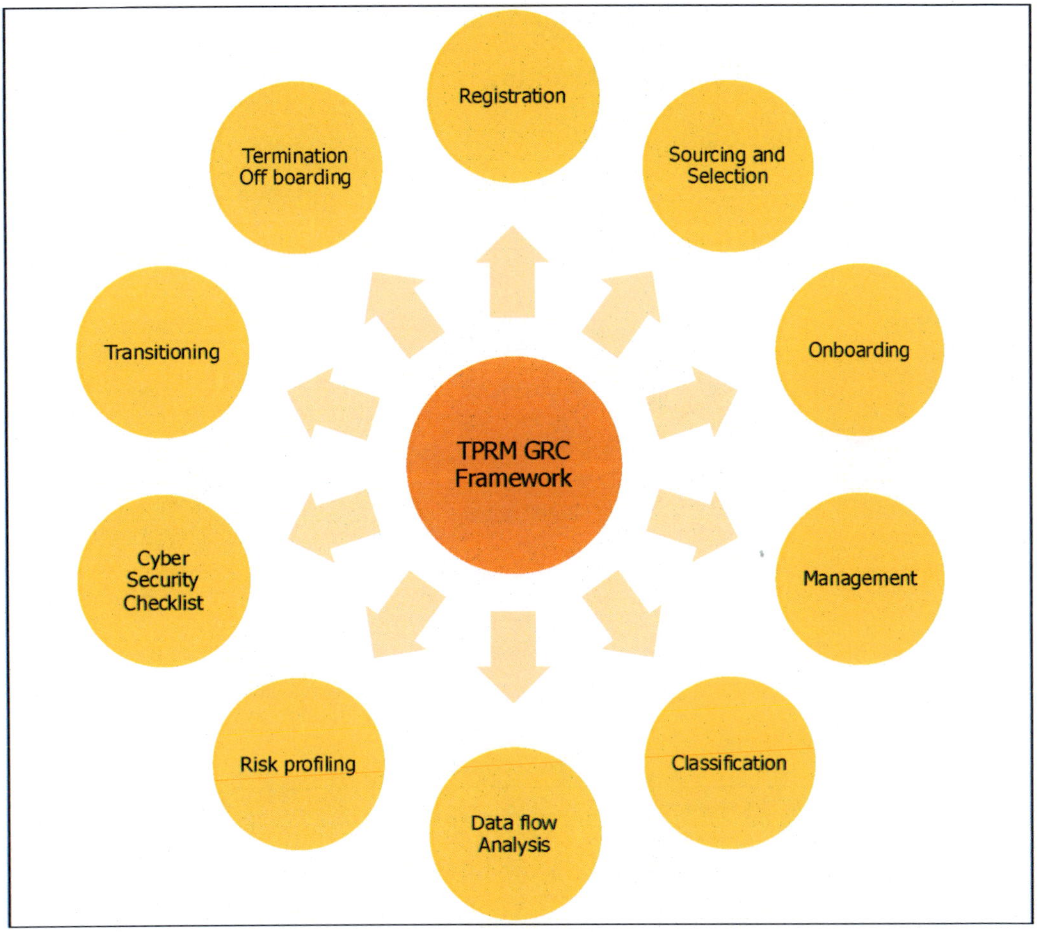

Figure 62 VRM Onboarding

Vendor Risk Management framework phases

- **Profiling the vendors**
  - Understand the vendor's services type
- **Categorization of the Vendors**
  - Map Vendor services to business needs

- **Audit Methodology**
  - o Build audit approach and methodology for each type of vendor profile
- **Monitoring and Reporting**
  - o Define KPI, measure, monitoring and report performance
- **Continuous improvement and Training**
  - o Service improvements, training

The phased approach towards the VRM framework is schematically presented below :

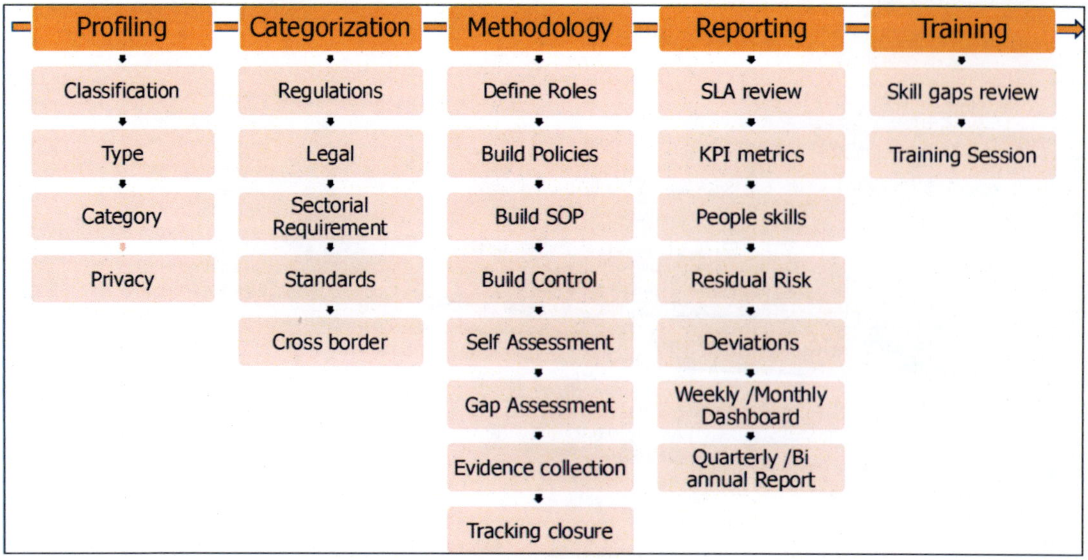

Figure 63 VRM framework An Approach for illustration

Depending on the **nature, type, and volume of vendors,** organizations must define an appropriate and scalable approach to their Vendor Risk Management (VRM) program. The implementation model can range from **manual, checklist-based processes to automated tools or web portal-driven solutions,** tailored to meet the organization's specific operational and compliance requirements.

For organizations managing a **large and diverse vendor base**-particularly those operating across multiple regions or business units-manual approaches may become inefficient and prone to errors. In such cases, adopting an **automated, smart template-driven or SaaS-based vendor management portal** can significantly enhance efficiency and oversight. A typical approach considers the following:

- Group vendors based on the type of services that are been supported
- Define the legal , procurement , HR requirements with respect to outsourced need
- Define the Data Security requirements to address information systems compliance requirements
- Build and document operational workflow and methodology , build templates for onboarding , managing, monitoring and subsequent deboarding so that it is in lines with organisational adopted practices
- Build awareness culture between vendor teams and different internal operations on the operating model
- Define the roles and responsibility of different teams who are going to be part of the business model
- Evaluate the requirement to deploy digital rights management platform for enhancement security

A sample template for initiating the build of VRM framework can include a basic information gathering sheet. The sheet helps to capture all information with the vendors, the service which is being provided ,the requirement of compliance if any and other details which can be customized to individual needs.

Vendor Name	Service Provided	Risk Classification	Due Diligence Performed (Yes/No)	Security Policies Reviewed (Yes/ No)	Vulnerability Assessment Conducted (Date)	Vulnerability Assessment Responsibility	Contract Security Clauses Included (Yes/ No)	Compliance with Data Protection Laws (Yes/No)
[Enter Vendor]	[Enter Service]	[High/Medium/Low]	[Yes/No]	[Yes/No]	[Date]	[Responsible Team]	[Yes/No]	[Yes/No]

Compliance with Data Protection Laws (Yes/ No)	Incident Reporting Clause Included (Yes/ No)	Audit Conducted (Date)	Issues Identified (Yes/ No)	Corrective Actions Taken (Yes/ No)	Next Review Date	Backup Taken (Yes/ No)	Backup Responsibility	Vendor Application/Service Details
[Yes/No]	[Yes/No]	[Date]	[Yes/No]	[Yes/No]	[Date]	[Yes/No]	[Responsible Team]	[Application/Service Details]

Figure 64 VRM data Collection Template

4. VRM Policy Template

The policy presented is a template of VRM which can be considered for reference. As per individual requirement it may be required to be customized and sections and clauses modified based on specific needs.

Objective:

Safeguard the organization from risks arising due to third-party vendors, service providers, or partners by ensuring they meet the organization's cybersecurity standards and maintaining continuous monitoring for compliance and security.

1. Scope

This policy applies to:

- All third-party vendors, suppliers, contractors, and service providers who have access to the organization's systems, data, or critical infrastructure
- All third-party agreements, contracts, and partnerships that involve handling sensitive or critical data
- Personnel responsible for Vendor Management, Compliance, and Risk Assessments

2. Policy Statements

2.1 Third-Party Risk Assessment

- **Due Diligence:** Assess the cybersecurity posture of all third-party vendors before onboarding to ensure they comply with industry best practices and relevant regulations
  - Evaluate security policies, practices, and incident response capabilities.
  - Conduct vulnerability assessments and security audits of third-party systems that interact with the organization's infrastructure.
- **Risk Classification:** Classify third parties based on the sensitivity and criticality of the data they handle, assigning appropriate levels of security controls based on risk
- **Ongoing Risk Monitoring:** Implement a continuous monitoring process to assess changes in the third party's cybersecurity stance, compliance, or risk level over time

2.2 Security Requirements in Contracts

- **Security Clauses:** Include specific cybersecurity and data protection requirements in all third-party contracts, ensuring that
  - The third party must implement appropriate security controls to protect the organization's data and systems

  - o The third party must notify the organization immediately in case of a security breach or incident
  - o Security measures must be maintained throughout the contract term, with periodic assessments and audits

- **Data Handling & Compliance:** Ensure contracts stipulate data protection obligations, such as data encryption, access control, and compliance with relevant laws (e.g., GDPR, PDPL, DPDPA and others)
- **Exit Strategy:** Define processes for securely ending relationships with third parties, including the return or destruction of data and assets

2.3 Vendor Audits and Assessments

- **Periodic Audits**: Conduct regular audits of third-party vendors to verify compliance with security requirements and identify potential vulnerabilities or risks. Audits may include vulnerability scanning, penetration testing, and review of access controls and data protection practices
- **Audit Frequency:** Set the audit frequency based on vendor risk classification, with high-risk vendors being audited more frequently.
- **Remediation Actions:** Document any gaps identified during audits and ensure that third-party vendors take corrective actions within specified timelines.

2.4 Incident Response and Collaboration

- **Incident Reporting:** Ensure third-party vendors are contractually obligated to report security incidents affecting the organization's data or systems within predefined timelines
- **Joint Incident Response:** Define a process for joint incident response efforts in case of a breach, ensuring collaboration between the organization and its third-party vendors to mitigate risk
- **Communication Plans:** Establish clear communication protocols between the organization and vendors during an incident to ensure transparency and coordination

Vendor Lifecycle Management

- **Onboarding Process:** Include cybersecurity assessments as part of the onboarding process for new vendors

- **Ongoing Management:** Continuously evaluate vendor performance and security posture throughout the lifecycle of the relationship, making adjustments as needed
- Offboarding: Securely manage the offboarding of vendors, ensuring proper data deletion or return and revocation of system access

2.5 Roles and Responsibilities

Vendor Risk Manager

- Conduct due diligence on third-party vendors and evaluate their cybersecurity posture
- Oversee the vendor onboarding and contract negotiation process to include security clauses
- Manage and coordinate periodic security audits and risk assessments of vendors

CISO

- Ensure alignment of all third-party risk management practices with the organization's overall cybersecurity strategy
- Review third-party security incidents and breaches to assess impact and implement corrective actions

Legal and Compliance Teams

- Ensure that third-party contracts include appropriate cybersecurity and data protection provisions
- Provide guidance on regulatory requirements regarding third-party risk management

IT Team

- Support risk assessments by conducting security reviews and vulnerability assessments of vendor systems
- Assist in monitoring third-party access to internal systems and data

Internal Audit Team

- Conduct audits of third-party risk management practices and vendor compliance with security standards
- Evaluate the effectiveness of security controls implemented by third-party vendors

5. Conclusion

In today's digital ecosystem, where data is continuously accessed, processed, and sub-processed by multiple third parties, **safeguarding organizational assets and sensitive information is paramount.** Vendors and third-party providers often gain privileged access to critical systems and confidential data, making it essential to **implement robust controls to prevent unauthorized access, misuse, loss, or replication** of information.

To ensure effectiveness, the **Vendor Risk Management (VRM) program must be closely aligned with the organization's Information Security Management System (ISMS).** This alignment promotes a **cohesive and structured approach** to managing risks associated with third-party engagements, thereby supporting secure and compliant operations.

Given that third-party dependencies are integral to modern business models, organizations must tailor their VRM implementation based on the **number, type, and criticality of vendor relationships.** Whether through manual processes, automated platforms, or integrated SaaS solutions, the objective remains the same-**to ensure vendors operate securely and in alignment with the organization's risk management and compliance expectations.**

A well-executed VRM program not only reduces risk exposure but also builds trust, enhances operational resilience, and supports long-term business sustainability.

Chapter

15

Key performance Indicators

1. Introduction

In today's digital landscape, the exponential increase in cyber threats has elevated **cybersecurity** to a strategic priority. Information system security is now a regular agenda item in boardrooms, with **global standards, regulatory bodies, and governance frameworks** placing greater emphasis on top management involvement.

Key Performance Indicators (KPIs) serve as essential tool to track, monitor, and evaluate the organization's cybersecurity posture. They enable organizations to assess progress towards its business objectives, risk management goals, and regulatory compliance while facilitating data-driven decisions.

At its core, a KPI provides a quantifiable metric that reflects the effectiveness, efficiency, and maturity of implemented controls. Timely review and reporting of KPIs help identify performance gaps, optimize resource allocation, and ensure continuous improvement of cybersecurity and resilience efforts.

2. Key Performance Indicators

Information Security Metrics: Turning Data into Insights

Information Security Metrics help transform raw security data into actionable insights that enable better decision-making. By tracking trends and presenting quantifiable data, these metrics provide visibility into an organization's vulnerabilities, strengths, and areas for improvement.

Effective dashboards and KPIs help communicate cybersecurity-related business risks to IT and executive stakeholders. They also illustrate the potential impact of cyber threats on an organization's reputation, operations, and regulatory compliance.

Purpose of Cybersecurity KPIs

Key Performance Indicators (KPIs) are designed to:

- Measure the effectiveness, compliance, and maturity of cybersecurity and cyber resilience controls
- Track security operations and risk mitigation efforts across key functional areas
- Enable real-time monitoring and performance assessment aligned with organizational goals and regulatory standards

Types of KPIs

KPIs can be classified into two main categories:

- **Executive or Management-Level KPIs**

  These indicators support high-level decision-making, risk reporting, and stratgic communication.

- **Operational or Technical KPIs**

  These focus on the daily effectiveness of security processes, controls, and technologies.

Guidance for Implementation

The KPIs presented here are generic and high-level. ,Organizations are encouraged to customize these KPIs based on:

- Business context
- Risk appetite
- Regulatory obligations
- Cybersecurity framework (e.g., ISO 27001, NIST CSF)

Regular review and enhancement of KPIs is essential to adapt to evolving threats and improve cyber resilience.

1. Incident Detection and Response

- **Mean Time to Detect (MTTD):** Average time taken to detect cybersecurity incidents after they occur
- **Mean Time to Respond (MTTR)**: Average time taken to respond to and mitigate an incident after detection

- **Incident Closure Rate:** Percentage of incidents that are resolved within the defined timeline
- **Post-Incident Review Completion Rate:** Percentage of incidents that undergo post-incident analysis and learning sessions

2. Asset and Inventory Management

- **Asset Coverage Rate:** Percentage of IT assets inventoried and classified correctly
- **Asset Audit Frequency:** Number of audits conducted on the IT asset inventory within a given time period (e.g., quarterly, annually)
- **Accuracy of Asset Inventory:** Percentage of assets identified in audits that match the documented inventory
- **Asset Utilisation:** Percentage of usage of assets for each type vs used stale/ obsolete assets

3. IT Access and Authorization

- **Access Review Frequency:** Number of access reviews conducted within a given period (e.g., quarterly, annually).
- **Unnecessary Access Revocation Rate:** Percentage of unnecessary or outdated access privileges revoked during reviews.
- **Access Control Violations:** Number of unauthorized access incidents reported within a period
- **Access provisioning:** Number of users added /deleted / unused etc

4. Change Management Process

- **Change Request Approval Time:** Average time taken for change requests to be reviewed and approved.
- **Change Success Rate:** Percentage of changes that are implemented successfully without incidents or downtimes.
- **Change-related to Incidents**: Number of security incidents failures directly related to recent changes
- **Roll back done**: Number of failed changes which required rollback

5. Acceptable Use Policy (AUP)

- The percentage of employees trained and compliant with the policy
- The number of policy violations detected and resolved,

- Adherence to log retention and review requirements,
- The effectiveness of access controls for restricted platforms.

6. HR Policy

- Focus on successful completion of screening ,onboarding processes,
- Compliance with policy training,
- Number of incidents reported related to unauthorized information dissemination,
- Proper handling of exit formalities,
- Adherence to monitoring and reporting mechanisms for employee behaviour

7. Business Continuity Management (BCP/DR)

- **BCP/DR Plan Testing Frequency:** Number of times BCP/DR plans are tested (e.g., annually)
- **Recovery Time Objective (RTO) Achievement:** Percentage of systems and processes recovered within the defined RTO
- **Recovery Point Objective (RPO) Achievement:** Percentage of systems and data restored within the defined RPO

8. Backup and Recovery Management

- **Backup Success Rate:** Percentage of successful backups conducted as scheduled
- **Backup Recovery Test Rate:** Percentage of backup restoration tests conducted and passed.
- **Backup Storage Redundancy:** Number of geographically dispersed backup locations used to store critical data

9. Third-Party Risk Management

- **Third-Party Risk Assessment Completion Rat**e: Percentage of third-party vendors assessed for cybersecurity risks.
- **Vendor Audit Frequency:** Number of vendor audits conducted within a given period.
- **Third-Party Incident Rate:** Number of cybersecurity incidents originating from third-party vendors.

10. Network & Communication Security

- **Network Segmentation Implementation Rate:** Percentage of critical assets placed in segmented network zones.
- **Encryption Compliance Rate:** Percentage of communications (email, data transfers) that are fully encrypted.
- **Security Event Detection Rate:** Percentage of suspicious activities detected by network security tools (firewalls, IDS/IPS).

11. Security Logging and Monitoring

- **Log Collection Coverage Rate:** Percentage of critical systems and applications that generate logs
- **Log Review Frequency:** Number of log reviews conducted within a defined period (e.g., weekly, monthly)
- **Incident Detection via Logs:** Percentage of security incidents detected through log analysis
- Number of usage case built with correlation
- Number of possible threats detected from threat intel feeds

12. Cyber Crisis Management

- **Crisis Plan Update Frequency:** Frequency at which the Cyber Crisis Management Plan (CCMP) is reviewed and updated
- **Crisis Simulation Participation Rate:** Percentage of key personnel participating in crisis management simulations and exercises
- **Crisis Resolution Time:** Average time taken to resolve a cyber crisis from initiation to final resolution

13. Application Security and Secure Application Development

- **Vulnerability Remediation Time:** Average time taken to address and remediate identified vulnerabilities
- **Penetration Test Coverage:** Percentage of applications tested via vulnerability assessments and penetration testing.
- **Secure Coding Violations:** Number of secure coding violations detected during application development
- **Vulnerabilities detected:** Percentage of critical , high , medium detected

14. Data Protection and Privacy

- **Data Encryption Compliance Rate:** Percentage of sensitive data that is encrypted both at rest and in transit
- **Data Privacy Incident Rate:** Number of incidents related to data privacy violations or unauthorized access
- **DPIA Completion Rate:** Percentage of Data Privacy Impact Assessments (DPIA) completed for new data processing activities

15. Endpoint Security

- **Endpoint Protection Coverage:** Percentage of endpoints protected by end point security tools such as EDR/AV
- **Patch Management Compliance:** Percentage of endpoints with up-to-date security patches
- **Endpoint Security Incident Rate:** Number of incidents caused by unprotected or compromised endpoints
- **End points user awareness**: number of issues which related to non-awareness of security controls

16. Data Leakage Prevention (DLP)

- **DLP Policy Violation Rate:** Percentage of detected policy violations related to data leakage
- **DLP Solution Coverage:** Percentage of critical systems and endpoints protected by DLP solutions
- **Sensitive Data Exfiltration Attempt Rate:** Number of attempts to exfiltrate sensitive data blocked by DLP systems
- **DLP incidents reports:** Number of DLP Incident reports vs incident where action taken and Number of false positive incidents

17. Email Gateway Security

- **Phishing Detection Rate:** Percentage of phishing emails successfully detected and blocked by email security solutions.
- **Spam Detection Rate:** Percentage of spam emails successfully filtered by email security systems
- **User Awareness Training Completion Rate:** Percentage of employees trained on email security best practices and phishing awareness

18. Cyber Audit and Compliance

- **Audit Completion Rate:** Percentage of scheduled internal and external audits completed on time
- **Compliance Issue Resolution Time:** Average time taken to resolve non -compliance findings from audits
- **Regulatory Compliance Rate:** Percentate of compliance with applicable regulatory requirements.

19. Risk Management

- **Risk Identification Time:** Average time taken to identify new risks
- **Risk Mitigation Time:** Average time taken to implement mitigation actions
- **Incident Response Time:** Average time to respond to risk-related incidents
- **Compliance Issue Resolution Time:** Average time taken to resolve non - compliance findings from audits
- **Regulatory Compliance Rate:** Percentate of compliance with applicable regulatory requirements.
- **Risk Reporting Frequency:** Frequency of risk reports submitted to management / board
- **Risk Appetite Breach Resolution Time:** Average time to address breaches of risk appetite limits

General KPIs for Cybersecurity Effectiveness

- **Cybersecurity Awareness Training Completion Rate:** Percentage of employees who have completed cybersecurity training programs
- **Security Awareness Program Participation:** Percentage of staff engaging in cybersecurity awareness campaigns or events.
- **Risk Mitigation Effectiveness:** Percentage of identified cybersecurity risks mitigated within the defined timeframe

The above list of KPI provided is more from management dashboarding, a similar granular level operational KPI which can build . One can use the different parameter as defined in the standard operation procedure to define operational KPI

3. KPI Report and Dashboarding methods

Organizations today utilize a number of methods to get the reports and management dashboard.

- Traditional approach is to get the data collected in excel based worksheets and then do sorting , filtering and trending and built custom charts and macros. This is very effective way and can be further integrated with reporting tools
- Dashboarding interface tools can be deployed further which has the capability to import inputs in multiple formats and provide rich reports with graphs and charts and also export in word /pdf or other formats
- Number of deployed tools also have an individual console interface to generate native reports, which can be integrated in to the centralized dashboarding tool for providing management reports
- Separate dashboards can be defined for Operational level KPI and Management level KPI
- Based on the automation deployed RBAC (role-based access control) can also be configured to give online status view to different stake holders

4. Conclusion and Summary

Key Performance Indicators (KPIs) play a vital role in shaping an organization's cybersecurity maturity and operational transparency. Their effective implementation leads to measurable outcomes that support both strategic and day-to-day decision-making.

KPI play a very important role -

- **Drive Organizational Maturity:** KPIs help measure the effectiveness of cybersecurity controls and build maturity in the organization's security posture
- **Enable Transparent Communication:** Serve as a communication bridge between management and operational teams, ensuring alignment on security goals
- **Improve Operational Efficiency:** Facilitate informed decision-making that leads to optimal utilization of IT resources and reduced downtime
- **Strengthen Cybersecurity Posture:** Provide quantifiable metrics to track adherence to regulatory, legal, and industry standards, reducing exposure to cyber threats
- **Support Performance Management:** KPIs can also serve as inputs for employee performance evaluations, offering valuable insights to Human Resources during appraisals and talent assessments.

Chapter

16

Understand Maturity Concepts in Security Operation Centre (SOC)

1. SOC basics

SOC Basics

A **Security Operations Centre (SOC)** is a centralized, 24x7 operational environment staffed by skilled **Information Security professionals** and **cybersecurity analysts.** The SOC is responsible for continuously monitoring the organization's IT infrastructure, including on-premises systems, cloud environments, endpoints, network devices, and applications.

Objectives of the SOC

The primary goals of a SOC are to:

- **Detect** security threats and anomalies in real-time
- **Analyse** the impact and scope of potential threats
- **Respond** rapidly to incidents and initiate containment or remediation
- **Coordinate** with appropriate internal teams (IT, network, application, etc.) for resolution
- **Ensure compliance** with regulatory and organizational security requirements

When a cyberattack or suspicious activity is detected, SOC analyst evaluate the incident based on **severity, criticality, and business impact.** The findings lead to the creation of an **incident ticket,** which is escalated to designated **resolver teams** for further action.

The SOC functions through various tools and processes-foremost among them is the **Security Information and Event Management (SIEM)** platform. SIEM enables the aggregation, normalization, correlation, and alerting of log data across the environment to facilitate incident identification and response.

Before exploring the workflow and maturity levels of a SOC, it is important to understand the **"Event-to-Incident Pipeline"**, which forms the foundation of SOC operations.

- All devices in the IT infrastructure generate different types of Events based on the activity which is being carried on the IT assets . The event activity can be system generated or user generated or a security related
- Event activity may result in audit Logs (messages) which are initially stored on the respective device and transfered to log management tools for analysis
- Log messages post monitoring , analysis by SOC analyst, gets converted in Alerts indicating of a possible suspicious activity by either internal or external users of the IT environment
- Alerts post reviewing the criticality and severity gets converted in Alarms indicated generally as Red-Amber-Green Status
- SOC analyst post triaging and confirming of a possible issue generates an Incident ticket with in the SOC tool platform, which is then forwarded to respective IT teams to resolve

The above flow of event to incident is presented in the schematic diagram below:

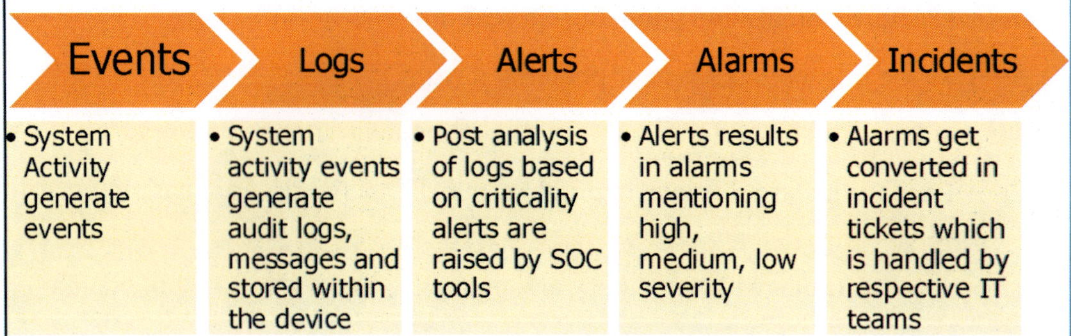

Figure 65 Incident pipeline

2. SOC framework

The basic building block of any SOC is circled around 3 areas ie. People, Process and Technology. All the areas are playing an important role in building a structured and robust operations center.

The following shows a schematic block diagram of typical SOC operations:

- People mean all the professionals ie SOC Analyst, Subject Mater Experts, CISO and other Information Security professionals who are working as part of the SOC,
- Process means all the operating policies, procedures which are defined for running day-to-day functions such as Service Level Agreements, response time to incidents, resolution time and others
- Technology includes all the Tools and technology platforms which is used in SOC to provide 24*7 monitoring and includes SIEM, SOAR, ITSM, DFIR, UEBA, NBAD, Threat Intel feeds and others

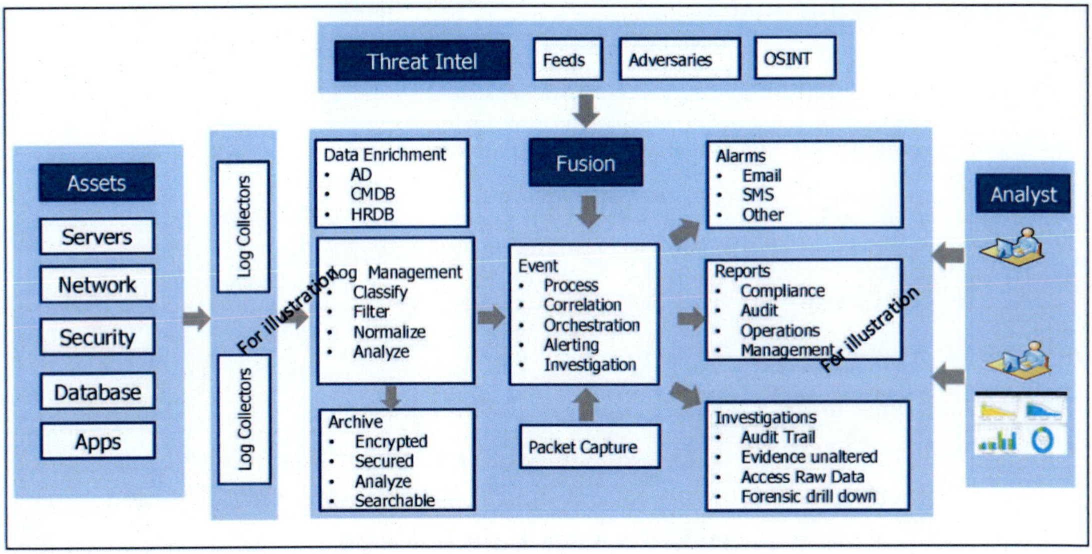

Figure 66 SOC Framework A View point

- **Assets** are all IT infrastructure systems servers, applications, Network devices, Security tools which have been deployed in the environment and are generating logs of different kinds

- **Log collector** is part of the log management function, which consolidates log data from all devices centrally which is further used for security event monitoring and analysis
- **Threat Intel Platform** aggregates, correlates, and analyzes threat data from multiple sources feeds in real time and gets ingested with log data in SIEM platform to help carry out analysis
- **Fusion** is where log data , threat data gets merged into the SIEM platform, which through its automation helps to process the events, correlate, and through in built automation does orchestration and generate alerts, alarms to respond to security incidents
- **Analyst** team are SOC professionals who are responsible for monitoring of events, responding to events and managing the SIEM platform, and managing the incidents

3. SOC Maturity operational model

SOC Maturity Operational Model

The maturity and effectiveness of a Security Operations Centre (SOC) depend on multiple factors, including:

- The **complexity of the digital infrastructure**
- The **geographic spread** of operations
- **Regulatory and standards compliance** requirements
- Availability of technical expertise to build, operate, and manage the SOC

In-house vs. Managed SOC

Organizations must make a strategic decision between establishing:

- An **in-house (on-premises) SOC**-which allows for full control but requires significant amount of investment in people, processes, and technology
- An **outsourced or Managed SOC (MSSP model)** - which offers scalability, cost-efficiency, and access to expert analysts, but with trade-offs in data residency and control.
- A hybrid model with on-premise tools and outsourced professionals to third party providers

This decision should align with the organization's risk appetite, budget, compliance obligations, and cyber resilience goals.

Cybersecurity Maturity Model for SOC

A Cybersecurity Maturity Model, aligned with **Capability Maturity Model Integration (CMMI)** principles, provides a phased roadmap to evolve SOC capabilities. It enables organisation to benchmark its current state and prioritize improvements across people, processes, and technologies.

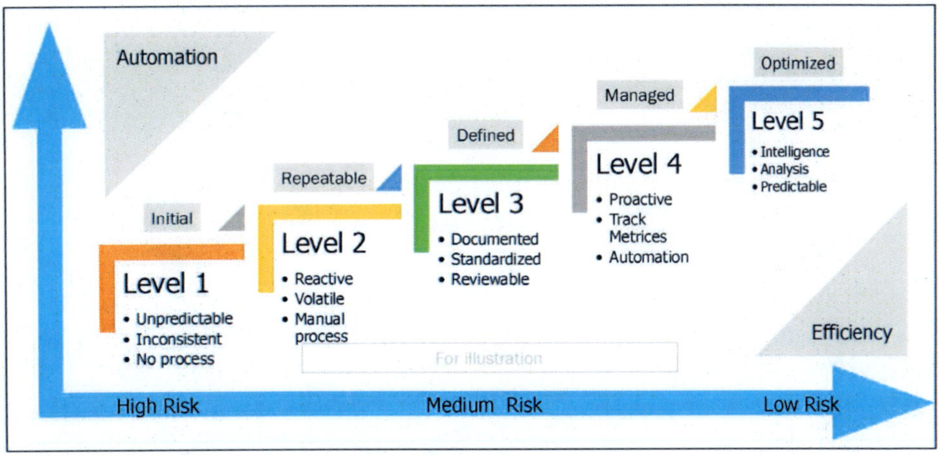

Figure 67 SOC Maturity Model

Each of the levels can be mapped indicating the current state of usage of standards and processes providing a view of the SOC operations effectiveness . The measure can thus help to determine the overall risk posture and possibly exposure to cyber threats

- **Level 1 - Initial:** No Processes or typically undocumented in raw unformatted manner and in a state of dynamic change, tending to be driven in an ad-hoc and uncontrolled manner
- **Level 2 - Repeatable:** Processes are repeatable but still reactive approach. Process discipline is unlikely to be rigorous
- **Level 3 - Defined:** Defined sets of standard processes and well documented subject to some degree of improvement over the period of time and in risk aware mode of operation
- **Level 4 - Managed:** Using process metrics, management can effectively control the processes and work in proactive manner
- **Level 5 - Optimize:** The focus is on continually improving process performance through both incremental and innovative technological changes or improvements are driven through intelligence and active feedback mechanism

Alternate Approach to Mapping SOC Security Posture: Technology Evolution Across Maturity Levels

Another effective way to understand and map an organization's SOC security posture is by analyzing how the **technology landscape evolves** as the SOC matures. This progression reflects a shift in operational focus and capabilities, typically moving through these stages:

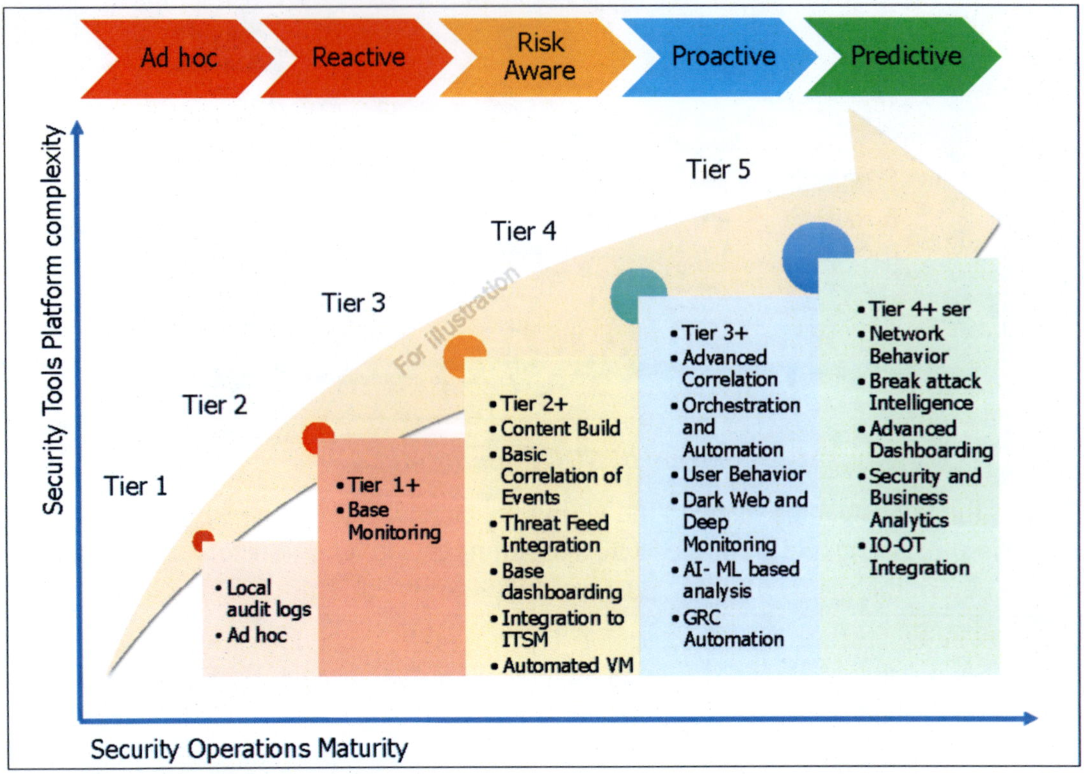

Figure 68 SOC Technology Maturity and Adoption RoadMap

- **Tier 1**
  - Standalone or tools deployed, log auditing may or may not be enabled
  - No formal monitoring or review of event logs is done.
  - Incident analysis is done on need basis. Firefighting mode of security deployment
- **Tier 2**
  - Basic logs from perimeter security devices such firewall, proxy etc is enabled and reviewed periodically, as part of security device administration and management.

  - Organisation are aware of the possible risks and threats but still working in reactive mode

- **Tier 3**
  - Reasonably aware of risks and threats to IT infrastructure from both internal and external users.
  - Have taken sufficient measures to implement security incident and event management tools .
  - Tools are integrated with default threat feeds and 24*7 monitoring SOC have been deployed at basic level.

- **Tier 4**
  - Incident monitoring has been integrated with different security tools and automation and orchestration has been deployed at initial level. High level of correlation has been implemented.
  - Multiple threats feed are being integrated for granular analysis . Advanced solutions such as attack surface intelligence, brand monitoring are being used to proactively identify and detect threats.
  - Apart from this organisation has also adopted GRCaaS concept and managing the GRC framework through used of AI tools

- **Tier 5**
  - This maturity is in advanced stage
  - All digital process, security technology have been considered for monitoring
  - AI-ML security analytics has been integrated with business analytics data to predict possible events which may lead to disruption of services

Details of specific solutions and services are beyond the scope of this document. The objective here is to present the conceptual understanding of how effective SOC management is pivotal in building and advancing an organization's security maturity.

Future-generation SOCs, when integrated with Vulnerability Management, Security Device Management, and GRC automation - all enhanced with embedded Artificial Intelligence (AI) capabilities - will be able to operate in near real-time. Such SOCs will not only identify and detect potential security threats but also take automated actions to respond to attacks, thereby preventing major disruptions to business operations.

This approach exemplifies the implementation of **"Contextual Security Intelligence"** - a paradigm shift from relying solely on static controls to actively preventing threats by continuously monitoring security events within their broader context. It is security that is adaptive, intelligent, and preventative rather than reactive.

Glossary of Terms

The following terms have been referred across various sections in the documents. The terms have been expanded for further reference. The terms and full forms are as per defined by respective bodies / standards / regulations.

- **NIST** – National Institute of Standards and Technology
- **ISO** – International Standards Organization
- **IEC** – International Electrotechnical Commission
- **CIS** – Center for Internet Security
- **ITGC** – IT General Controls
- **COBIT** - Control objective for IT
- **IoT – IIoT** – Internet of Things , Industrial Internet of Things
- **Industry 4.0** – Fourth Industry Revolution (AI, Big Data)
- **Industry 5.0** – Fifth Industry Revolution
- **ISO27001** – Information Security Management System Standard of ISO
- **ISO27701** – Privacy Information Management Standard of ISO
- **ISO42001** – Artificial Intelligence Management System of ISO
- **ISA/IEC 62243** – Operational Technology Standard
- **ISO22301 BCMS** – Business Continuity Management System Standard of ISO
- **ISO 9001** – Quality Management System Standard
- **ISO 20000** – IT Service management standard
- **IRDAI** – Insurance and regulatory Authority of India
- **RBI** - Reserve Bank of India
- **SEBI** – Securities and Exchange Board of India
- **UIDAI** – Unique Identification Authority of India
- **UPI** – Unified Payment Interface
- **Cert-In** – Computer Emergency Response team – India Body

- **MOD** – Ministry of Defence
- **ISNP** – Insurance Self Networking Platform
- **NCIIPC** – National Critical Information Infrastructure Protection Centre
- **DOT** – Department of Telecom
- **HKMA** – Hong Kong Monetary Authority
- **MAS** – Monitory Authority of Singapore
- **NESA** – National Electronic Security Alliance UAE
- **SAMA** – Saudi Arabian Monetary Authority
- **PCI-DSS** – Payment Card Industry Data Security Standard
- **NBFC** – Non-Banking Financial Companies
- **DPDPA** – Digital Personal Data Protection Act
- **SOC 2** – Service Organisation Controls
- **HIPAA** – Health Insurance Portability and Accountability Act
- **CMMC** – Cybersecurity Maturity Model Certification
- **C2M2** – Cyber Capability Maturity Model
- **FAIR** – Factor Analysis of Information Risk
- **GDPR** – General Data Protection Regulation
- **BPIA** – Business Process Impact Assessment
- **DPIA** – Data Privacy Impact Assessment
- **BCP** – Business Continuity Plan
- **ITDR** – Information Technology Disaster Recovery
- **ITIL** – Information Technology Infrastructure Library
- **IPC** – Incident Problem Change Management
- **CMDB** – Configuration Management Data Base
- **DAST** – Dynamic Application Security Testing
- **SAST** – Static Application Security Testing

- **IAST** – Interactive Application Security Testing
- **SOP** – Standard Operating Procedures
- **DAST** – Dynamic Application Security Testing
- **SIEM** – Security Incident and Event Management
- **SOAR** – Security Orchestration and Response
- **ITSM** – IT Service Management
- **DFIR** – Digital Forensic and Incident Response
- **UEBA** – User Entity Behaviours Analysis
- **NBAD** – Network Behaviour Anomaly Detection

Disclaimer: The documents have reference to different global and regional standards, regulations , frameworks as mentioned in the glossary. We have also referred few other sources as a guide while drafting different areas of the book. All illustrations, tables presented are provided to give a generic viewpoint on the authors thoughts around the concepts. All templates of policy, standards operating procedures provided are for establishing the concepts around respective sections and will need customization to meet respective regional requirements . The book is purely as knowledge sharing document to help professionals understand GRC and enhance skills around the subject.

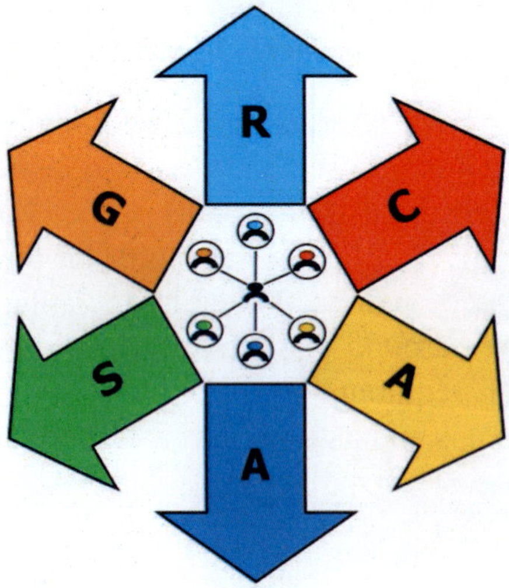

GRC As A Service